This book
BELONGS TO

_____

A Good Meal

IS **HARD** TO **FIND**

A Good Meal

IS HARD TO FIND

Storied Recipes from the Deep South

Amy C. Evans & Martha Hall Foose

CHRONICLE BOOKS

SAN FRANCISCO

Library of Congress Cataloging-in-Publication Data:
Names: Evans, Amy C., author, illustrator. | Foose, Martha Hall, author.
Title: A good meal is hard to find : storied recipes from the deep South / Amy C. Evans and Martha Hall Foose.
Description: San Francisco : Chronicle Books, [2020]
Identifiers: LCCN 2018042967 | ISBN 9781452169781 (hc : alk. paper)
Subjects: LCSH: Cooking, American--Southern style. | Cooking--Southern States. | LCGFT: Cookbooks.
Classification: LCC TX715.2.S68 E9 2020 | DDC 641.5975--dc23 LC record available at https://lccn.loc.gov/2018042967

Manufactured in China.

Design by Kelley Galbreath and Lizzie Vaughan.

10 9 8 7 6 5 4 3 2 1

Chronicle books and gifts are available at special quantity discounts to corporations,
professional associations, literacy programs, and other organizations.
For details and discount information, please contact our corporate/premiums department
at corporatesales@chroniclebooks.com or at 1-800-759-0190.

Chronicle Books LLC
680 Second Street
San Francisco, California 94107
www.chroniclebooks.com

DEDICATIONS

For my grandmother, Alla Grace Browder Riley;

my mother, Mary Ann Riley Evans;

and my daughter, Sofia Grace.

—Amy

For my mother, Cynthia Yandell Vaughan Foose,

with admiration and love.

—Martha

TABLE OF

Contents

Foreword

AMY, THE PAINTER

I STARTED MAKING PORTRAITS OF THE LADIES, as I like to call them, back in about 2006. I remember being in my Oxford, Mississippi, studio, working on one of my usual still life paintings of vintage objects, when it occurred to me: What if I created a story to go with these crazy collections of seemingly mismatched things? I had never been interested in giving my work anything more than simple descriptive titles before that moment, but it started to make sense that dreaming up a story for my quirky picture puzzles would add another dimension to them—and offer up a good reason for a few petit fours to appear in the same painting as a can of hairspray.

As soon as I committed to the idea, the stories spilled out like buttons from a jar. Later on in the series, as I began painting on bigger panels, I started to include vintage fabric patterns in the composition as a way to set a lady's life story in a particular era. After a while, I managed to amass a motley cast of characters that spanned generations. Strong women who don't mind eating alone and can do for themselves. Quirky

gals who have oddball habits and are stuck in their ways. Good talkers who like to eat cake for breakfast and will gladly accept the offer of a well-considered cocktail. It turns out that The Ladies are an awful lot like the women I get to call my friends.

One of those strong-willed, food-loving, super-hospitable friends is Martha Foose. On one of my visits to Martha's home in Greenwood, Mississippi, I walked into her kitchen, and there was a half-eaten strawberry cake on the counter. It didn't take but a minute for us to sit down at her kitchen bed, as she calls it (a generously padded banquette that anchors two sides of her breakfast table), to enjoy hefty slices of pink cake, along with jelly jars of bourbon to wash them down. I haven't the slightest idea what time of day it was. It could very well have been midmorning or midnight. What I do know is that sitting in Martha's kitchen is one of my very favorite places to be, and it's where I spent many hours over the course of our collaboration on this book.

Martha and I first met in Greenwood, probably sometime during the summer of 2003. I was in town to document area restaurants. Martha had recently returned to the Delta to open a bakery. I would bet money that it was her cousin LeAnne who first introduced us. However it happened, Martha and I got on like a house on fire. And I fell in love with the town of Greenwood, too. I loved it so much that I got married there in 2005. Martha made my wedding cake. It was red velvet, and I never tire of sharing the eye-popping tidbit that Martha used sixteen bottles of food coloring to achieve the perfect shade of oxblood. My marriage didn't stick, but our friendship did.

All told, I lived in Mississippi for thirteen years. I called the university town of Oxford home for all of that time, but I took a Delta ramble every chance I could. And I still do. I moved back to my hometown of Houston, Texas, in 2014, but I keep returning to Mississippi because it is my soul place. It is the place where I feel most connected to the land and the people, the food and the stories.

I had just moved back to Houston when Martha and I were swapping stories on the phone one afternoon, and she happened to mention that she always thought that the titles of my paintings would make great recipe headnotes. She never came right out and said that she wanted to be the one to make a book with me, but she definitely planted the seed. I can be a bit bullheaded, so it took me a while to come around to the idea that we—a painter and a cook—could actually collaborate on a book. When I called her up a little more than a year later, asking if she would want to do a book like that with me, she was quick to say yes.

When my daughter, Sofia, was born, Martha's aunt Lucy (LeAnne's late mama) gave her a string of pearls because, she said, every Delta girl needs one. Sofia hasn't worn them yet, but she sure knows where they came from. And I can say the same for the stories in this book. I know that they came from the generations of women who raised us and fed us and told us stories and were glad when they finally got to sit down and put their feet up for a spell. The friends who gathered together for all of life's celebrations. The women who leaned on each other and summoned a laugh in hard times. The ones who have leftover cake and a glass of bourbon for breakfast when no one's watching.

Here's to you, ladies.

MARTHA, THE COOK

I'VE GOT AN OLD COMMUNITY COOKBOOK I found at an estate sale that has the combination of a safe written in immaculate, sharp-penciled script right under a recipe for Mrs. Munson's Cold Tongue. It read, "Turn Left to 18, Turn Right to 32," and so on. The first thing I did when I came upon this inscription was phone up Amy and send along a picture of the yellowed page. It was just the sort of thing that makes us swoon.

I've spent most of my days on this earth in kitchens as a waitress, baker, chef, cooking school instructor, cookbook writer, wife, and mother. What keeps me intrigued, I've come to realize, is the language of flavor.

The essence of a dish tells a story. Some can be comfortingly intimate, and others are surprisingly new. Stringing together words, like seasoning a dish, should be done with care. Bitter, salty, sweet, and peppery connote different tones and characterize different qualities of ingredients. The sharpness of vinegar brings an edge of bitterness, though it should be kept in check. Sweet words to one held dear like apricot jam can be cloying if not tempered with a bit of saltiness to keep things real.

I am drawn to the gratifying ritual of day-to-day meals and have a reverence for passed-along recipes. The superstitions of cooks and strong-held beliefs of diners never cease to amaze me. The recital of anecdotes while pots are bubbling, the narration of instruction when recipes are passed along, and how the quality of ingredients should be as high as the sincerity of words will keep me in the kitchen.

Once Amy and I set out in earnest to write this book, we spent so much time with the characters from her paintings and the ones we had newly conjured up, it seemed we had populated an entire community of souls with opinions and tastes of their own. Many of the recipes contained in this album are rooted in the vintage cookbooks we covet. Some are based on the backstories of the subjects in Amy's paintings and the mementos they collected. We imagined and invited new community members to share their prized possessions, secret thoughts, and favored recipes. Some are tributes to real folks we love. Many times it appeared that The Ladies and their companions ferried us into their neighborhood and pulled up a stool for us at their kitchen counter.

Amy has an astonishing talent for getting to the heart of a matter through a visual shorthand. What I have found is that her generous spirit enables others a chance to tell their stories, too. Each brushstroke, like every stir and sprinkle, adds to these storied recipes.

Introduction

THE FIRST TIME MARTHA AND I GOT TOGETHER to work on this book, we sequestered ourselves at her farmhouse in Pluto, Mississippi, the spot of land in the Delta that Martha's family has called home for generations. Since Pluto is seventeen miles from the one place where you can get not much more than a gallon of milk, some Nabs, crickets, and a quart of motor oil, we packed for every contingency. Martha even brought along her cotton candy machine to entertain my daughter, Sofia. Sitting at the dinette table in the kitchen, looking out onto the Delta landscape, we began to conjure up the gang of women you meet here. We discussed their lives and their loves, their favorite finger foods and their foibles. The clubs they belonged to and the groups that they wouldn't dare be associated with. Who wouldn't care to take the time to make a pie dough, and who has a taste for baby corn. We even got nitpicky about how these ladies take their coffee and what they keep on their bedside tables. Somehow, as we said their names aloud—Esther, Ouida, Josephine—they emerged from the ether and appeared as fully realized women.

Maybe it is part of our personalities, perhaps it is part of being Southern, or perhaps it is just something in the Delta air, but Martha and I have always shared a certain affinity for oddball characters. We are both drawn to people who can make a way out of no way and stick to their guns. Some might call it stubbornness or steadfastness, but we call it moxie. But we are sentimental fools, too. When Martha visited the Downtown Greenwood Farmers Market one Saturday morning and bought fresh onions from Hallie Streater, a farmer from Black Hawk, Mississippi, whom I got to know when I interviewed her in 2011, she immediately texted me a picture: three plump little onion bulbs tied together with a strand of red yarn done up in a bow. It is details like this that make our hearts flutter.

We are also intrigued by consumerism—the things people buy and sell, what they keep and what they discard. How a throwaway matchbook can become the keepsake of a lifetime. Martha and I both require regular doses of resale shop–therapy, visiting estate sales, and rummaging through other people's forgotten trinkets and treasures, on the hunt for stories.

These are some of those stories. And like Pauline's* charm bracelet that overfloweth, we choose to share them with you. We hope they inspire you to throw a casserole in the oven, invite some neighbors over, and get to sharing some stories of your own.

YOUR FRIEND,

Amy

---

* Do try Pauline's Lucky Pickle Relish Dogs on page 62.

**OUR COMMUNITY IS
PRACTICALLY BOUND
BY MAYONNAISE**

DUCHESS'S MAYONNAISE

◆◆◆

MAKES A HEAPING CUP

1 large egg

1 large egg yolk

1 Tbsp distilled white vinegar

1 Tbsp freshly squeezed
lemon juice

1 tsp fine sea salt

1 tsp dry mustard powder

Pinch of cayenne pepper

½ cup canola oil

½ cup avocado oil

TO MAKE WITH AN IMMERSION OR STICK BLENDER: Put your egg and yolk, vinegar, lemon juice, salt, mustard, and cayenne in a wide-mouth pint jar. (Large jars help reduce splatters.) Stand your immersion blender up in the jar. Slowly pour your oils over the eggs.

Hold your blender tight against the bottom of your jar and give it a few pulses at low speed until the mixture begins to turn creamy and opaque at the bottom. Continue to slowly pulse with the blender touching the bottom, jostling the blender around a bit, for a few seconds, or until the mayonnaise begins to thicken. Plunge the blender up and down only until well combined.

TO MAKE IN A FOOD PROCESSOR OR TRADITIONAL BLENDER: Double all of the ingredients because many blenders and food processors are too large to effectively emulsify your mayonnaise. Combine your oils in a liquid measuring cup.

In the bowl of a food processor or blender pitcher, pulse your egg and yolk, vinegar, lemon juice, salt, mustard, and cayenne until well combined.

With the machine running, drizzle in your oils in a very slow, steady stream until the mixture thickens and begins to turn opaque and all of the oil is incorporated.

This can be stored in the refrigerator for a few days.

Morning's GLORIES

Pearl's
WISH

➤➤➤ ❋ ◄◄◄

MAKES EIGHT DRINKS

One and a half 12 oz cans
(2¼ cups) evaporated milk,
well chilled

⅓ cup light rum, or to your liking

1 Tbsp light brown sugar

¼ tsp vanilla extract

4 cups pellet ice or crushed ice,
divided

1¼ cups freshly squeezed
orange juice, strained to
remove any pulp, well chilled

Mandarin orange sections
for garnish

PEARL SPIKED HER DRINK. Sunbathing in an almost-too-comfortable fold-out chaise, Pearl focused on the warm sun seeping through her eyelids. It was her first vacation in forever, and she'd made a point to take this one alone. After another sip of her newly arrived poolside concoction, Pearl sat up, took in the scenery around her, and decided she'd hunt up a realtor before the dinner bell chimed.

~~~~~~~~~~~

TAKE A LARGE PITCHER and stir together your evaporated milk, rum, brown sugar, and vanilla until the sugar has dissolved. Add 2 cups of your ice. While continually stirring, slowly add the juice in a slow, steady stream. Serve in tall glasses over ice garnished with mandarin orange sections.

NOTIONS & NOTES
◆◆◆

IT IS CRUCIAL FOR THE EVAPORATED milk and orange juice to be cold, cold, cold. And you must be patient and consistent when adding the orange juice to the milk or you risk the chance of it curdling.

AN INSULATED PITCHER OR CARAFE keeps these drinks nicely chilled for serving.

PELLET ICE IS OUR FAVORITE type to use in this Orange Julius–like drink. You can buy it by the bagful at Sonic Drive-In.

MANY DOMINICANS ARE FOND of the drink Morir Soñando, which combines fresh juice and some type of milk or cream. This concoction was inspired by the many renditions of the drink found throughout the Caribbean islands. The name translates to the romantic phrase "to die dreaming."

IF YOU WOULD LIKE TO DRESS this drink up a little more, float half a shot of Cointreau on the surface of each glass. Adding a festive paper straw makes the drink even more enjoyable.

Marge's
USUAL SUNRISE

⟫⟫✳⟪⟪

MAKES ONE COCKTAIL

1 tsp kosher salt

1/8 tsp chili powder

6 oz freshly squeezed pink
grapefruit juice

Crushed ice

1 jigger (1 1/2 oz) honeysuckle vodka

NOTIONS & NOTES

◆◆

CATHEAD DISTILLERY
Established in 2000, Cathead
Distillery is home to the oldest
legal still in Mississippi.
We support their directive
printed on each bottle:
Support Live Music.

MARGE HAD HER USUAL BREAKFAST AND THEN SHE TOOK HER USUAL MEASUREMENTS. For her, those usual measurements included two fingers of flower-scented vodka and four inches of her beloved pink grapefruit juice. Marge's ex-sister-in-law opened her pantry, saw all the rows of Texsun lined up neatly, and called her a creature of habit. That did not sit well with her. Why, just today, Marge added chili powder and salted the rim of her glass. That was most unusual.

〰〰〰

ON A SMALL SAUCER, combine your salt and chili powder. Moisten the rim of a tall glass with a bit of the grapefruit juice and then dip the rim of the glass in the salt and chili mixture to lightly coat the rim. Fill your glass with crushed ice. Add the vodka, then the grapefruit juice.

MAKE YOUR OWN
HONEYSUCKLE-FLAVORED VODKA

Steep 1/2 cup fresh honeysuckle blossoms
with the green leaves removed in 2 cups unflavored vodka
and 1 Tbsp sugar for 24 hours. Strain and store in a
capped bottle or jar in the refrigerator for a few days.

TEXSUN

pink
GRAPEFRUIT JUICE

PARIS FEED COMPANY   PARIS, TX.

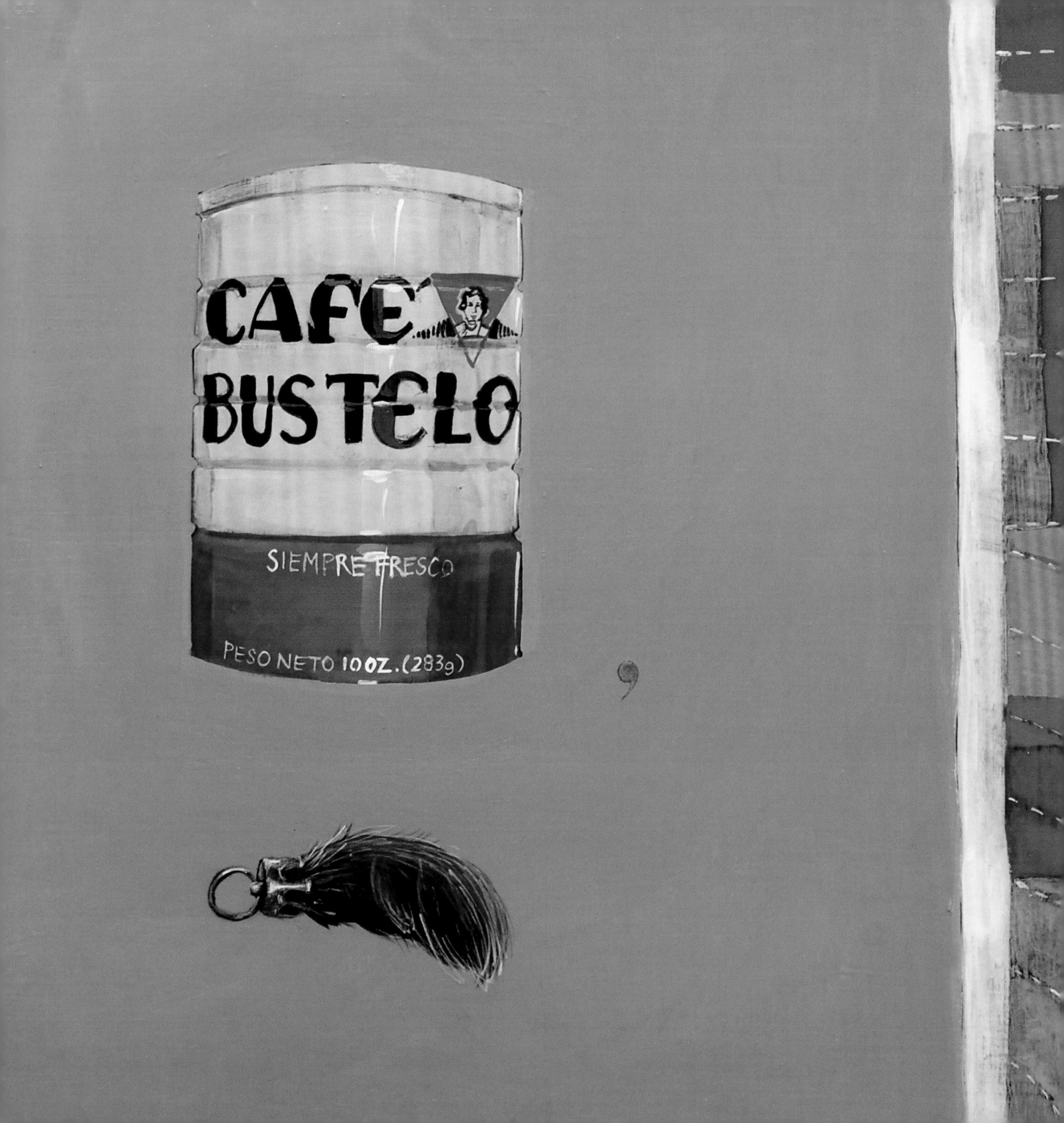
CAFE
BUSTELO
SIEMPRE FRESCO
PESO NETO 10 OZ. (283g)

Loretta's
CAFÉ CON MITAD Y MITAD

MAKES FOUR SERVINGS OF SPICED COFFEE

1 Tbsp unsweetened dark cocoa powder

1 Tbsp granulated unrefined cane sugar

Tiny pinch of ground cinnamon or small piece of cinnamon stick

1 quick grate of whole nutmeg

1/2 cup half-and-half

4 cups strongly brewed hot coffee

THE NEIGHBORS WERE ARGUING AGAIN, SO LORETTA TOSSED AWAY THE COVERS, GOT UP, PUT ON HER ROBE, AND HEADED TO THE KITCHEN. She recalled last night's garden party and that handsome stranger who poured her a glass of punch. She just couldn't get him off of her mind. Loretta put the coffee on the stove and then crawled back into bed to find the details of her dreams.

WHISK your cocoa powder, sugar, cinnamon, and nutmeg together in a small pot. Whisk in your half-and-half. Heat over low heat until as hot as desired. Add your coffee and serve.

CAFÉ BUSTELO

was founded in East Harlem in 1928 by Gregorio Bustelo, a Spanish émigré. It is a robust, rich, espresso-style coffee. The can it comes in, with its Art Deco–style label, is a favorite recycled vessel among artists of all types, but painters in particular.

Dolores's
VIBRANCY WATER

━━━ ➤➤➤ ❋ ⬤⬤⬤ ━━━

MAKES FOUR DOSES

3 cups cold water

½ cup roughly chopped cucumber

½ cup roughly chopped, peeled
fresh or frozen mango

1 Tbsp freshly
squeezed lime juice

2 tsp muscovado sugar

⅛ tsp hot paprika

Pinch of fine sea salt

EVERY MORNING, DOLORES PUT HOT PAPRIKA IN HER WATER AND CUCUMBERS UNDER HER EYES. Her husband, Ventura, told her each and every morning that she was as beautiful as the moment he had first laid his eyes on her. That was in Manila, Christmas Day, 1942. She believes that this morning constitutional, coupled with other secret concoctions, keeps her vibrant.

〜〜〜〜〜〜〜〜〜〜〜

IN A QUART JAR, combine your water, cucumber, mango, lime juice, sugar, paprika, and salt. Shake well. Chill and serve. You can keep this drink in your refrigerator for up to 3 days.

TO REDUCE PUFFINESS, apply chilled half moons of cucumber beneath your eyes while sipping this restorative morning elixir.

NOTIONS & NOTES

◆◆◆

MUSCOVADO SUGAR

is a soft, moist, strongly molasses-tasting dark cane sugar produced in the Philippines and Mauritius. Aside from retaining the flavor of the cane juice, the sugar also keeps its mineral content of phosphorus, calcium, magnesium, potassium, and iron. Muscovado sugar is widely available online and in specialty baking shops.

Ouida's BUTTERED PIMIENTO SOUFFLÉ

——→→ ❄ ←←——

MAKES SOUFFLÉ FOR SIX

One 2 oz jar sliced pimientos, drained

¼ cup (½ stick) unsalted butter, at room temperature

10 slices hearty white sandwich bread, crusts removed

2 cups whole milk

4 large eggs

8 oz sharp Cheddar cheese, divided

½ tsp dry mustard powder

¼ tsp freshly grated nutmeg

Dash of Worcestershire sauce

Generous pinch of salt

OUIDA, IF NOTHING ELSE, WAS UPBEAT. Good Morning, Sunshine! She'd make the same salutation to her parakeet Rufus each and every morning, no matter the weather. She had that bird trained to start a morning song in return. But if it were soufflé-making day, Ouida would keep Rufus's cage covered and hum quietly to herself along with the blender.

ARRANGE AN OVEN RACK in the center position of your oven with no rack above it. Heat your oven to 325°F. Put your pimientos on paper towels to absorb the excess juice. Lightly butter a 2-quart ceramic soufflé or round baking dish. Then lightly butter each slice of your bread. Cut the buttered bread into 1-inch chunks. Put your milk and eggs in a blender and pulse to combine. Add the bread and half of your cheese to the blender, pushing it down into the milk and eggs. Pulse the blender a few times and then give the contents a stir to rearrange them. Add your mustard, nutmeg, Worcestershire sauce, and salt. Blend some more, until you have a smooth batter. Pour your batter into your buttered dish. Sprinkle your remaining grated cheese over the batter and gently fold it into the batter. Sprinkle your pimientos over the top.

BAKE YOUR SOUFFLÉ at 325°F for 60 to 65 minutes, until it is a deep golden color and puffed up in the center. Serve posthaste!

NOTIONS & NOTES

•——◆◆◆——•

GRATE THE CHEESE YOURSELF
on the large-holed side of a box grater for best results. Shredded packaged cheese is often mixed with cellulose to keep it from clumping together. This substance, which is derived from wood pulp, will, as you might imagine, have an adverse effect on your soufflé.

THIS MAKES AN AWFULLY GOOD DINNER WITH A SALAD ON THE SIDE.

Dot's
SWEET POTATO AND BACON PURSE PIE

MAKES A DOZEN SMALL POCKETBOOK-SIZE PIES

1 cup mashed baked sweet potato

1 Tbsp cane syrup

1 large egg, beaten

3 tsp ground allspice, divided

3 bacon slices, cooked until very crisp and crumbled

One 14.1 oz package refrigerated pie dough

Vegetable oil for frying

⅓ cup granulated unrefined cane sugar

EXTRA

When you bake your sweet potatoes, throw in an extra or two to make Ivy's Sweet Sausage Balls (page 32).

AFTER ARRIVING HOME IN THE MORNING, STILL IN HER EVENING ATTIRE, DOT MADE A QUICK CHANGE INTO A SHIRTWAIST, WASHED HER FACE, AND COMBED HER HAIR. Dot was running late, so she threw her breakfast in her purse and headed out the door. The Carondelet streetcar waits for no one.

IN A MEDIUM BOWL, combine your sweet potato, cane syrup, egg, and 1½ tsp of the allspice. Fold in your bacon.

ON A LIGHTLY FLOURED WORK SURFACE, roll each piece of dough a bit thinner than it arrives out of the package. Cut out four 4½-inch rounds of dough from each piece. Gather the scraps, roll again, and cut four more rounds.

DIVIDE THE FILLING EVENLY among the rounds by placing 1 heaping Tbsp of filling a little off-center on each. Fold the dough over the filling and, using the tines of a fork, press the edges to seal them. Work carefully to press out any air pockets as you seal the edges of your pies.

WHEN YOU'RE READY TO FRY YOUR PIES, heat 1 inch of oil in a deep skillet to 350°F. Put your sugar and the remaining 1½ tsp allspice in a bag and shake it up.

PLACE THE PIES, TWO AT A TIME, in the hot oil and fry for 2 minutes per side, or until deep golden brown and crisp. Remove the pies from the oil, allowing any excess oil to drain back into the skillet. Gently flip each fried pie around in the bag with the allspice-sugar. Wrap each cooled pie in waxed paper.

NOTIONS & NOTES

THESE PURSE PIES
are a true joy to have on hand. Finished pies can be frozen and reheated in a 350°F oven for 20 minutes, or until warmed through.

CANE SYRUP
is made from boiled-down sugar cane juice and is not to be confused with molasses, which is a by-product from making granulated sugar. It has a lighter, sweeter, less sulfur-ish flavor than molasses. We like Alaga (which stands for Alabama and Georgia) and Steen's brands, which are widely available, but we are devoted to Leo Beatty's syrup from Louin, Mississippi.

WHEN STRAWBERRIES ARE COMING IN,

make a quick jam by cooking down 2 pints chopped hulled berries

and ½ cup sugar, a grating of nutmeg, and a little bit of fresh lemon

juice. You will end up with about 1¾ cups of deliciousness. Let it

cool completely, then store it in the refrigerator for a week or so.

Ethel's
OVERNIGHT BREAKFAST IN BED

➤➤➤ ❄ ⬅⬅⬅

**MAKES A SWEET
BREAKFAST FOR SIX**

4 cups cubed multigrain oat bread

½ cup top-quality strawberry jam
(see Note)

One 14 oz can sweetened
condensed milk

1 cup half-and-half

6 large eggs

1 tsp finely grated
orange zest

½ cup sliced natural almonds

1 cup sliced fresh strawberries
or other berries, if desired

Powdered sugar for dusting,
if desired

ETHEL LOVED BREAKFAST IN BED. Too bad she had to make it for herself. In an effort to feel like there was a regular someone who did nice things for her to make her feel beloved, she always set the ingredients together the night before. When she settled back underneath the covers with breakfast cooling on the bed tray before her, she imagined her beau away at work and planned the night's supper for two.

〜〜〜〜〜〜〜〜

BUTTER an 8-by-11½-inch (2-quart) casserole dish and put your bread cubes inside. Spoon tablespoon-size dollops of jam over the bread.

IN A MEDIUM MIXING BOWL, whisk or blend together your sweetened condensed milk, half-and-half, eggs, and orange zest until very well combined. Pour this mixture over your bread and jam. Sprinkle the almonds over the top. Poke the bread down into the custard, if needed. Spray or brush some aluminum foil with oil and cover the casserole. Refrigerate for 1 hour or overnight.

WHEN READY TO BAKE YOUR CASSEROLE, remove it from the refrigerator and heat your oven to 375°F. Keep the dish covered and bake for 40 minutes, or until the custard is slightly set. Uncover and bake for 10 minutes more, or until the almonds are toasted and the custard has puffed up and set. Scatter the strawberries over the top and dust with powdered sugar, if you like.

Francine's STRAWBERRY-GLAZED DOUGHNUTS

—»»» ❄ ««—

MAKES ABOUT TWO DOZEN
SMALL DOUGHNUTS

DOUGHNUTS

1 cup plus 2 Tbsp
whole milk, heated to 110°F

1/4 cup granulated unrefined
cane sugar

1 package (2 1/4 tsp)
instant yeast

2 large eggs, beaten

10 Tbsp (1 1/4 sticks)
unsalted butter, melted

4 cups unbleached
all-purpose flour

3/4 tsp fine sea salt

Vegetable oil for frying

GLAZE

2 cups powdered sugar, sifted,
plus additional for coating
doughnut holes

1/4 cup whole milk

1/2 tsp vanilla extract

1/4 tsp fine sea salt

One 0.8 oz package freeze-dried
strawberries, finely crushed

Rainbow jimmies, if desired

THE EVER-INDUSTRIOUS FRANCINE SET THE DOUGH TO RISE SHORTLY AFTER SHE DID. As proprietress of Francine's Beautique, everything fell to her. Her regulars had come to expect her homemade doughnuts at their standing appointments. After a full day of rinse-and-sets, Francine always ate a doughnut before going to bed. She thought it made her dreams sweet.

TO MAKE THE DOUGHNUTS: Put your milk, granulated sugar, and yeast in the large bowl of an electric mixer fitted with the paddle attachment. Mix on low speed for 1 minute, or until the sugar is dissolved. Add your eggs and butter. Mix on low until just combined. With your mixer running on low, add your flour and salt. Mix on low for 5 minutes, or until the dough clings to the beater and pulls away from the bowl. Take your dough out of the bowl. Oil the bowl lightly, return the dough to the bowl, and cover with a damp tea towel. Refrigerate the dough for 1 hour or up to 8 hours.

WHEN YOU ARE READY TO SHAPE YOUR DOUGHNUTS, generously flour two large rimmed baking sheets. Turn your dough out onto one of the sheets. Pat and roll your dough to a 1/2-inch thickness. Cut out your doughnuts with a 2 1/2-inch doughnut cutter, dusting lightly with flour as needed. Place your doughnuts and holes at least 1 inch apart on the floured baking pans. Cover with a slightly damp tea towel or food wrap. Let rise in a warm place until the doughnuts are puffed up and hold an indention when lightly poked with your finger, about 2 hours. This is a good time to make your glaze.

TO MAKE THE GLAZE: In a medium bowl, whisk your powdered sugar, milk, vanilla, and salt together. Whisk in your strawberries.

WHEN YOU ARE READY TO FRY YOUR DOUGHNUTS, set a wire rack over a pan to cool the doughnuts after frying and catch the drips after glazing. Heat at least 3 inches of oil to 370°F in a heavy, deep pot over medium heat or a deep fryer. Fry your doughnuts in batches of two or three. The doughnuts will sink for a few seconds, then bob to the surface. Fry for about 1 minute. Then use chopsticks, a slotted spoon, or a spider to turn the doughnuts and fry for another minute, or until beautifully golden with a pale belt around the sides. Cool slightly on the rack. Fry your doughnut holes, turning them with a slotted spoon. Cool slightly on the rack.

WHILE YOUR DOUGHNUTS ARE STILL WARM, DIP THE TOPS IN YOUR GLAZE. Return the doughnuts to the rack to cool and let your glaze set. Sprinkle with jimmies, if desired. Drizzle the doughnut holes with glaze or sprinkle with powdered sugar.

WE LIKE THE ATECO BRAND
2½-inch doughnut cutter.
A biscuit cutter coupled with
the large end of a decorative
icing tip to cut the center holes
works well, too. But who says
doughnuts have to be shaped
like a tire? Cut out any shapes
you like and fry them up.

**IF THE GLAZE SEEMS
TOO THICK,**
do not add more liquid. Instead,
warm the glaze over low heat,
stirring until it is looser. Try
all different types of crushed
freeze-dried fruits in your glaze,
like mango or apple. Make sure
the label clearly says "freeze
dried," not merely dried.

Ivy's
SWEET SAUSAGE BALLS

---*»»»* ❄ *«««*---

MAKES FOUR DOZEN BALLS

3 cups baking mix (such as Bisquick or your own, see Note), plus a little for dusting

$\frac{1}{2}$ tsp crushed fennel seed

6 oz ($1\frac{1}{2}$ cups) grated Monterey Jack cheese

1 lb sweet Italian sausage (casings removed)

1 cup mashed baked sweet potato

NOTIONS & NOTES

---◆◆◆---

THESE SAVORY SNACKS are a nice addition to a brunch buffet or given as a hostess gift.

IVY PACKED HER SUITCASE FOR THE TRIP. Seems she was on the road just about every week now, so she made sure to carry at least one tin of sardines, along with a batch of her signature sausage balls, both of which fit neatly in her car's glove box. She found that her choice of sustenance made for great conversation. Customers from Wilmington to Abilene have asked Ivy to share her secrets. She hasn't yet.

~~~~~~~

HEAT YOUR OVEN TO 375°F. In a large bowl, mix all your ingredients together until very well combined using your hands or an electric mixer fitted with the paddle attachment. Dust your work surface with a little baking mix. Divide your dough into four equal pieces. Form each piece into a long rope. Cut each rope into twelve pieces. Roll the pieces into balls and place them at least 1 inch apart on baking sheets. Bake at 375°F until the sausage is fully cooked and the balls are a deep orange and crisp on the bottoms, 20 to 25 minutes. Serve warm or at room temperature.

IF YOU WANT OR NEED TO MAKE THESE WITHOUT STORE-BOUGHT BAKING MIX

Spin 3 cups flour, $1\frac{1}{2}$ Tbsp baking powder, 2 tsp salt, and $\frac{1}{2}$ cup shortening in a food processor for a few seconds, or cut the shortening in with a couple of forks until it is really mixed in with the flour.

Ruby's
RED-EYE GRAVY

❯❯❯ ❄ ❮❮❮

SERVES FOUR TO SIX FOLKS

2 Tbsp unsalted butter,
at room temperature, divided

2 tsp unbleached
all-purpose flour

One 1 lb center-cut country ham
slice (cut in pieces, if needed,
to fit in the skillet)

1 cup strongly brewed
black coffee

3 Tbsp tomato ketchup

White rice grits (see Note),
hominy grits, or biscuits for serving

TRIPP COUNTRY HAMS

in Brownsville, Tennessee,

produces some fine country

hams. They will even send them

right to your front door.

If you give them a ring at

1-800-471-9814, you can ask

for whole hams, slices,

or biscuit-size pieces.

RUBY READ THE NOTE AGAIN WHILE HER COUNTRY HAM WAS IN THE SKILLET AND THEN QUICKLY REFOLDED IT AND TUCKED IT AWAY WHERE PRYING EYES WOULD NEVER SEE. After putting the ham on a plate, she pondered promises broken and tipped her coffee into the drippings. If only everything came together as simply as a gravy.

〜〜〜〜〜〜〜

IN A SMALL BOWL, using a fork, mix 1 Tbsp of your butter with the flour and set it aside to thicken your gravy after you cook your ham.

HEAT A BIG SKILLET OVER MEDIUM HEAT. Add your remaining 1 Tbsp of butter to the skillet. When the butter has melted, add your ham. Cook the ham for 2 to 3 minutes on each side, or until it begins to brown and curl up slightly. Remove the ham from the skillet and set it aside until your gravy is ready.

TO MAKE YOUR GRAVY, pour the coffee into the skillet and scrape all the browned bits from the bottom of the pan. Add your ketchup and ¼ cup water. Cook and stir your gravy for 2 minutes, until very bubbly. Add that little bit of flour and butter you saved and mix it in with a fork. Let the gravy come to a boil. Lower the heat to medium-low and simmer for 3 minutes, stirring occasionally. Return your ham to the skillet, then flip it over to coat with the gravy. Serve over piping-hot white rice grits, hominy grits, or biscuits.

NOTIONS & NOTES

◆◆◆◆◆◆

MAKE A FEW SLITS
in any fat around the edges
of larger pieces of country
ham to keep it from curling
too much when it cooks.

ALWAYS, ALWAYS BE SURE
to thoroughly dry your cast-iron
skillets. We return them to a hot
oven or heat on the stove until dry.
We also moisturize our skillets
after each use with a spot of oil
wiped on with a paper towel. A
well-cared-for cast-iron skillet will
last through generations of use.

RICE GRITS
are what are termed "middlins,"
broken pieces of rice.

TO COOK RICE GRITS, *heat 1 Tbsp unsalted butter in a saucepan with a lid over medium heat until it melts. Stir in 1 cup rice grits, making sure they get thoroughly coated in the butter. Add 2 cups water or vegetable broth and a generous pinch of salt. Bring to a boil, stir, cover, and turn the heat to low. Simmer for 15 minutes, or until the water is all absorbed. We like Delta Blues rice grits from Ruleville, Mississippi, and Anson Mills rice grits out of Columbia, South Carolina.*

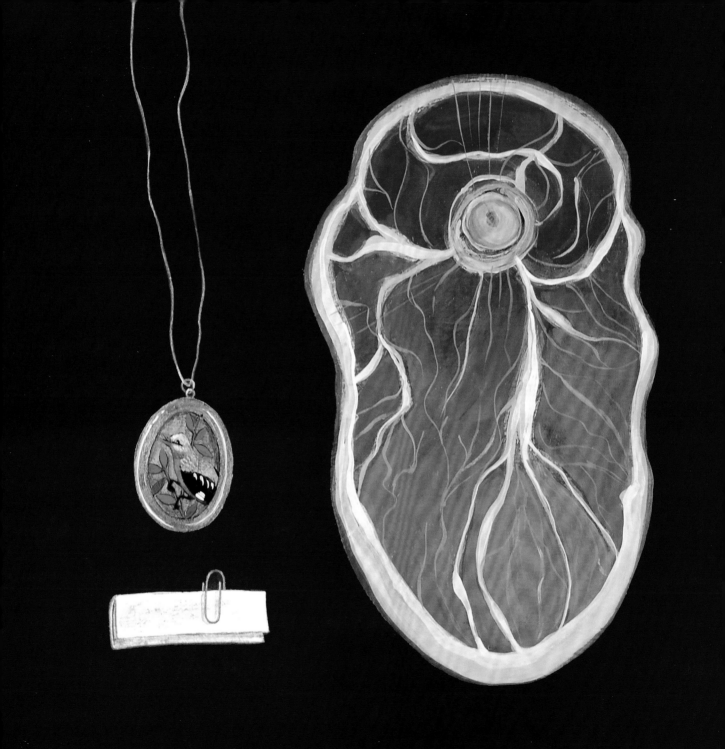

Carrye's
SUGAR / LUMP BISCUITS

——→→→ ❄ ←←←——

**MAKES A DOZEN
LEMON-FILLED BISCUITS**

2½ cups self-rising flour,
plus more for dusting

1 Tbsp granulated unrefined cane
sugar

1 lemon, zested and juiced

½ cup (1 stick) top-quality
unsalted butter, cut into
tiny pieces, chilled, plus 2 Tbsp
melted, divided

1 cup cold buttermilk

24 sugar cubes

CARRYE PREFERRED THAT TASTE OF TART OVER SWEET AND ALL THE THINGS YOU FIND AT THE FIVE AND DIME. She loved the way her hands smelled like candy after grating the rind off lemons to make her signature biscuits. In the heart of each one was a tart lemon surprise that drew lips into a pleasing pucker.

HEAT YOUR OVEN TO 475°F. Line a big baking sheet with parchment paper, aluminum foil, or a silicone baking mat.

IN A MEDIUM BOWL, combine your flour, granulated sugar, and lemon zest. Using a pastry blender, two forks, or your fingertips, cut the chilled butter into the flour until the butter is in very tiny pieces and evenly dispersed. Add the buttermilk and stir with a fork to form a tacky dough.

LIGHTLY FLOUR A SPOT ON THE COUNTER TO WORK. Turn your dough out onto it. Briefly and gently knead the dough until it is no longer shaggy. Pat the dough into a 9-by-5-inch rectangle. Fold the dough in half; roll and pat again until the dough is a rectangle ¾ inch thick. Very lightly dust the dough with flour. Using a sharp knife, cut 24 square biscuits. Place the biscuits on the lined baking sheet with the edges just barely touching. That way, they can help each other rise up nicely.

FOR EACH BISCUIT, dip one sugar cube into your lemon juice and poke it down into the center of the biscuit until the top of your sugar cube is just even with the top of the dough. Bake the biscuits at 475°F for 15 minutes, or until the sugar cube begins to bubble and the biscuits are risen and a lovely golden color. Remove the biscuits from the oven and brush the tops with your melted butter. Serve warm.

NOTIONS & NOTES

—◆◆—

WE ADORE the deep molasses flavor La Perruche Rough Cut Brown Sugar Cubes lend to the tart lemon centers of these biscuits. Of course, plain old white sugar cubes will do just fine.

Arturo's BUTTERMILK POPPY SEED WAFFLES WITH PLUM JELLY BUTTER

MAKES SIX BELGIAN-STYLE WAFFLES OR EIGHT THIN WAFFLES

2 cups unbleached all-purpose flour

2 Tbsp granulated unrefined cane sugar

2 tsp baking powder

1 tsp baking soda

1½ tsp poppy seeds

½ tsp fine sea salt

1 tsp finely grated lemon zest

2 cups buttermilk

14 Tbsp (1¾ sticks) salted butter, melted and kept warm, plus 8 Tbsp (1 stick), at room temperature, divided

2 large eggs

¼ tsp almond extract

¼ cup plum jelly

Sliced fresh plums, if desired

ARTURO TOOK A BREAK FROM THE SUNDAY CROSSWORD TO MAKE BREAKFAST. As he buttered his waffle, he puzzled over the answer for 24-down: a six-letter word for a type of root or meal.

"The meanings of words are serious things, you know," Arturo said . . . after talking all day, he was thirsty for buttermilk. —Eudora Welty, *The Shoe Bird*, 1964

IN A LARGE BOWL, WHISK TOGETHER YOUR FLOUR, sugar, baking powder, baking soda, poppy seeds, salt, and lemon zest. In a medium bowl, whisk together your buttermilk, melted butter, eggs, and almond extract. Now whisk the buttermilk mixture into your flour mixture just until you have a lumpy batter. Cover your bowl with a damp tea towel and let the batter sit for 20 minutes.

MEANWHILE, STIR TOGETHER your plum jelly and room-temperature butter and set it aside.

WHEN YOU'RE READY TO MAKE YOUR WAFFLES, heat your waffle iron to high and your oven to 200°F so that you can keep all the waffles warm as you make them, or leave the oven off and just dole them out as they are ready.

BRUSH OR SPRAY THE HOT WAFFLE IRON LIGHTLY WITH OIL. Waffle irons come in all shapes and sizes. Ours is a thick Belgian-style waffle maker, so we use a heaping ½ cup batter. Use what works with your iron. Cook your waffles until the steaming just about stops and the waffles are deep golden brown, 4 to 6 minutes. Put your cooked waffles on a rack in the oven to keep warm, if you wish. Don't stack them on top of each other because they'll turn soggy if you do that. Serve these with a good-size slather of the plum jelly butter. You are welcome to garnish with slices of fresh plums, if you have them handy.

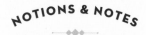

NOTIONS & NOTES

LETTING YOUR BATTER SIT for 20 minutes allows the flour to absorb the buttermilk and your leavening agents to get to work.

IF YOU PREPARE YOUR ingredients the night before by mixing the dry and having your eggs and buttermilk ready, the only thing to do in the morning is fool with the butter.

THESE WAFFLES FREEZE beautifully and are easy to heat back up in the toaster or oven on hurried mornings.

WE LIKE TO HAVE THESE poppy seed waffles as a savory snack sometimes. In that case, we mix equal parts butter and chow-chow relish to spread over the warm waffles.

IF YOU FIND YOURSELF in Jackson, Mississippi, take some time to visit Eudora Welty's home and gardens on Pinehurst Street.

THE SIX-LETTER WORD for a type of root or meal is *square*.

BUTTER

MILK

Dictiona

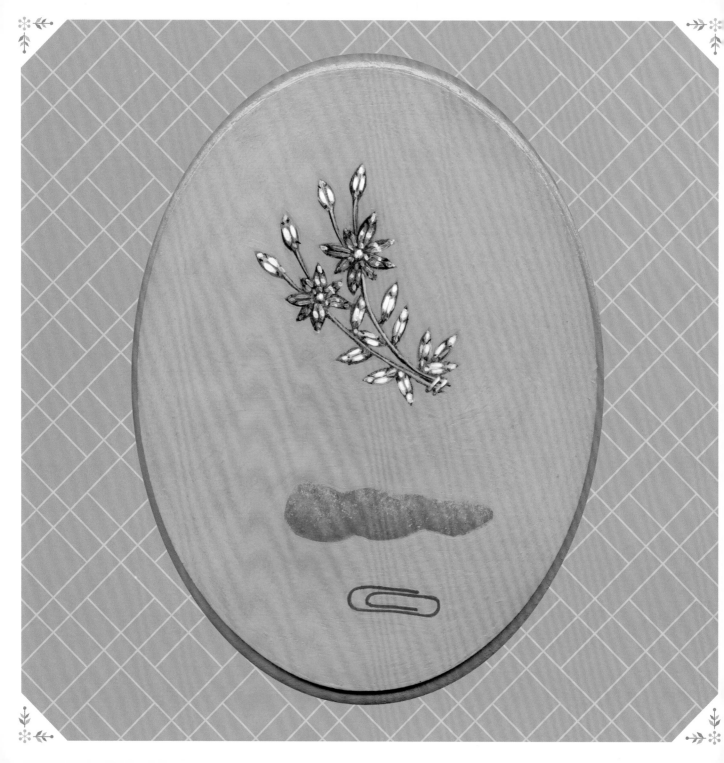

LINGERING
Lunches

f.

Bottled Sunshine

Sun Spot

© 1938

2

Nora's
HIBISCUS SODA POPS

MAKES SIX SODA POPS

4 cups white grape juice

¾ cup dried hibiscus

Ice for serving

1 L sparkling mineral water

EVENTUALLY, BOTTLED SUNSHINE JUST WASN'T GOOD ENOUGH. Nora had a taste for something new—something that tasted like spring smells. She walked out of her kitchen door and into the garden, on the hunt for inspiration.

IN A STAINLESS-STEEL POT OVER MEDIUM-HIGH HEAT, bring your grape juice to a boil. Turn down the heat and simmer until the juice has reduced by half, about 15 minutes. Remove from the heat and stir in your hibiscus. Let steep for 10 minutes. Strain though a fine-mesh strainer into a jar and discard the hibiscus. Chill the juice.

FOR EACH SODA POP, fill a large glass with ice. Pour ¼ cup of your juice over the ice and top with mineral water.

LOOK FOR

dried hibiscus in the tea section at the market or in Latino groceries. While you are there, keep an eye out for Topo Chico, a popular brand of mineral water that was first bottled in Monterrey, Mexico, in 1895 and can now be found all over the United States. Texans, and surely others, might sneak a nip of tequila in their hibiscus soda pop.

NOTIONS & NOTES

YOU CAN KEEP
this grape and hibiscus syrup in the refrigerator for about a month.

Rita's
ROADSIDE ATTRACTION

❋

MAKES DRINKS FOR FOUR

One 12 oz can frozen limeade concentrate, thawed until slushy

Three 12 oz bottles Mexican pilsner-style lager, very cold

½ cup vodka, chilled

4 lime wedges for garnish

RITA'S NAILS WERE STILL WET, SO SHE ASKED CARLA TO GRAB THE BOTTLE OPENER. The sun was about to set, and their end-of-the-dock perch offered up a million-dollar view. How they looked forward to their annual girls' trip! This time, though, Carla could've done without that call from home. Rita did her best to keep her friend's mind occupied with other things.

CHILL YOUR SERVING GLASSES IN THE FREEZER. Pour the limeade concentrate, beer, and vodka into a large pitcher, stir, and serve in frosted glasses. Garnish each glass with a wedge of lime.

NOTIONS & NOTES

◆◈◆

WE LIKE TO SERVE THESE DRINKS WITH
Clementine's Crawfish Puppies Dipped in H-Town Queso (page 90) and Gayle's Lucky Chicken Posole (page 55).

WE USE

Modelo Especial and Cathead Original Vodka in our version, but any brands will do. Serve in frosted pint glasses for extra-special guests.

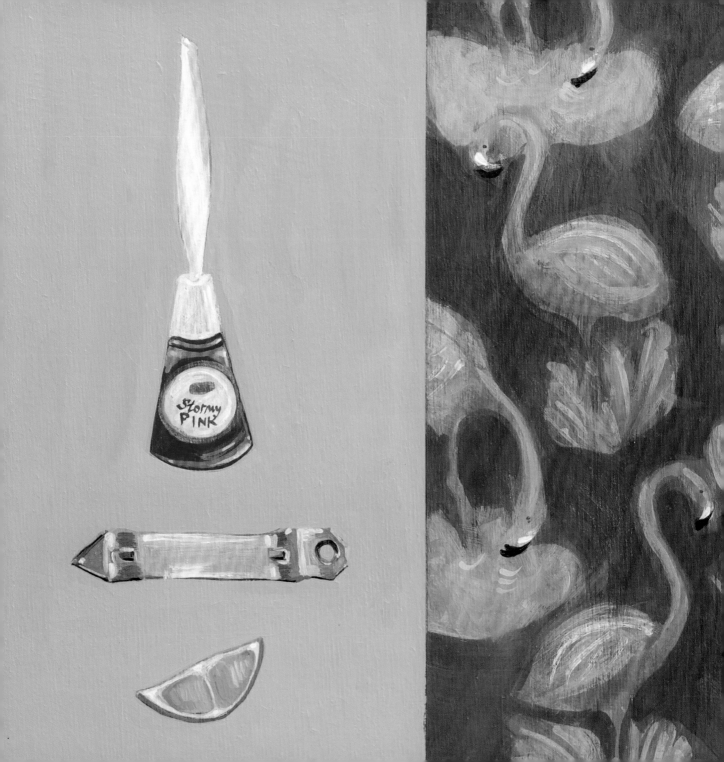

Nanaline's
SEAFOOD COCKTAIL OVER RED ICE

→→→ ❄ ←←←

MAKES FOUR APPETIZERS

NANALINE COVETED HER GRANDMOTHER'S ALUMINUM WARE THAT SHE KEPT AT THE BEACH HOUSE. Well, everything but those devilish ice cube trays. Even Gramma Marjorie called them widow makers, so Nanaline devised other uses for them. She placed the trays in drawers of her vanity to hold her cosmetics, and the sectioned inserts were perfect for cutting tea sandwiches for her monthly book club.

---

2 cups tomato and clam juice cocktail

Hot pepper sauce

1 Tbsp dry Louisiana crab boil seasoning

1 lemon, thinly sliced

½ lb (21 to 30 count) dry-packed sea scallops (about 12)

½ lb (21 to 25 count) peeled shrimp (about 12)

¼ lb cooked blue crab cocktail claws

NOTIONS & NOTES

⬩◆⬩

YOU MIGHT AS WELL freeze the rest of the bottle of Clamato into ice cubes, as they add the perfect chill to a Bloody Mary and will not water down your cocktail.

YOU CAN USE the poaching liquid in soups or gumbo.

IF YOU PEELED THE SHRIMP yourself, add those shells to the poaching liquid to fortify it.

MARINADE

½ cup freshly squeezed lime juice

¼ cup freshly squeezed lemon juice

¼ cup finely chopped green onions, both white and tender green parts

2 garlic cloves, finely chopped

2 Tbsp very finely chopped celery

2 Tbsp finely chopped fresh flat-leaf parsley

1 Tbsp finely chopped fresh oregano

1 Tbsp extra-virgin olive oil

2 tsp kosher salt

1 tsp granulated unrefined cane sugar

½ tsp coarsely ground black pepper

●━━━━━ ━━━

LOOK FOR

blue crab cocktail fingers labeled "pasteurized" in the seafood market. Many fishmongers will also steam fresh claws right in the store.

FILL AN ICE CUBE TRAY with the juice cocktail and add a dash or two of hot sauce to each cube. Freeze until solid. You might want to also chill your serving glasses now.

WHEN IT IS TIME TO COOK YOUR SCALLOPS AND SHRIMP, ready a large bowl of ice water. Submerge a colander in it to cool the seafood after poaching. Bring 1 quart water, the crab boil seasoning, and lemon slices to a boil in a nonaluminum pot. Lower the heat to a simmer. Add the scallops and let them poach for 1 to 2 minutes, or until just cooked through. Scoop the scallops out of the water with a slotted spoon and place them in your ice bath. Remove the pot from the heat and place the shrimp in the hot water. Keep a close eye on them. When they turn pink and curl ever so slightly, scoop them out and add them to the ice bath with the scallops. As soon as the seafood has cooled, remove the colander from the ice bath and let the seafood drain while you make your marinade.

TO MAKE THE MARINADE: In a large storage container (not a bag because the crab claws will poke holes in it), stir together all of the marinade ingredients. Add your scallops, shrimp, and crab claws to the marinade. Cover and let the seafood marinate in the refrigerator for 2 to 4 hours.

WHEN READY TO SERVE, pop the red ice cubes out into a bag and crush them. Spoon some of the crushed ice into four chilled, stemmed serving glasses. Drain the seafood and discard the marinade. Divide your seafood among the glasses by arranging about three of each type over the rosy crushed ice. Serve at once.

Alice's
ROSARY CANNELLINI SALAD

›››❄‹‹‹

**MAKES SALAD FOR
SIX TO EIGHT**

1 large red bell pepper

1 large yellow bell pepper

1 poblano pepper

Three 15 oz cans cannellini beans, drained and rinsed

4 oz very thinly sliced soppressata, cut into very thin strips

6 Tbsp extra-virgin olive oil

4 Tbsp sherry vinegar

1 Tbsp freshly squeezed lemon juice

1 tsp fine sea salt

1 Tbsp very finely chopped fresh rosemary

1 Tbsp very finely chopped fresh oregano leaves

¼ cup chopped fresh flat-leaf parsley

2 small heads of radicchio, cored and torn into bite-size pieces

ALICE PORED OVER THE LAST INSTALLMENT OF *AN ITALIAN ROMANCE.* She was so glad she saved up enough of her tip money to finally get the "Loyal Reader" subscription. Except that now, Alice thought of Guillermo every time she prayed the rosary or cooked cannellini beans, which happened at least twice a week.

PREHEAT YOUR BROILER. Put your peppers on a rimmed baking sheet and broil, turning occasionally, until charred on all sides, 6 to 8 minutes. Set the peppers aside to cool, reserving the juices on the baking sheet.

IN A BIG BOWL, combine your beans and soppressata. When cool enough to handle, pull the charred skin and seeds from the peppers and discard. Cut the peppers into thin strips and add to the beans. Pour any juices from the baking sheet over the salad. Drizzle the oil, vinegar, and lemon juice over the salad and sprinkle with the salt, rosemary, oregano, and parsley. Toss to combine everything. Let the salad marinate for an hour or so.

PLACE THE RADICCHIO on a large, deep serving platter and top with your bean salad. Serve at room temperature.

NOTIONS & NOTES

JARRED ROASTED PEPPERS are fine to substitute and are always handy to have in the pantry. And you can substitute jarred pepperoncini for the poblano pepper, too, on that kind of a day.

Camille's
BRIDGE CLUB EGG SALAD

—»»» ❄ «««—

SERVES A FOURSOME

7 hard-boiled or steamed eggs, peeled

⅓ cup very finely chopped celery stalk and leaves

1 green onion, both white and tender green parts, very finely chopped

¼ tsp finely ground white pepper

¼ tsp fine sea salt

½ cup Duchess's Mayonnaise (page 13) or store-bought mayonnaise

1 Tbsp store-bought yellow mustard

NOTIONS & NOTES

—◆◆◆—

TO DRESS UP
dainty egg salad finger sandwiches on party rye, put a tiny dot of mayonnaise on the top of each sandwich and stick a little celery or parsley leaf on each one.

CAMILLE'S GRANDMOTHER LOVED DUKE'S MAYONNAISE AND COSTUME JEWELRY. Given the right crowd, she could pass them both off as the real thing. She was quite a hand at Duplicate Bridge, although she preferred Rubber. When Camille was cleaning out the kitchen drawers in preparation for the dreaded estate sale, she found one of her grandmother's old scorecards with overtrick points and slam bonuses charted on one side and an egg salad recipe on the back.

～～～～～～～

CUT YOUR EGGS IN HALF AND CRUMBLE THE YOLKS INTO A MEDIUM BOWL. Add the celery, green onion, white pepper, salt, mayonnaise, and mustard. Grate the egg whites on the large-holed side of a box grater. Fold the whites into your yolk mixture.

TO STEAM YOUR EGGS

Place your eggs in a steamer basket set over boiling water. Cover and cook for 12 minutes. Meanwhile, fill a bowl with ice water. When the eggs are done, run them under cold water until they are cool enough to handle. Give each egg a crack and submerge them in the ice water until thoroughly chilled, 15 to 20 minutes. Peel the eggs under cold running water. For the love of all that is holy, do not overcook your eggs.

GAMBINO'S BAKERY, with locations in Baton Rouge and New Orleans, will ship a case of muffaletta bread to your doorstep.

NOTIONS & NOTES

USE THE REMAINING BREAD CRUMBS in place of, or in addition to, the panko in Agnes's Squash Blossoms (page 112).

IF YOU WANT TO MAKE YOUR OWN pickled beets, follow the instructions for making Pauline's relish (page 62), but replace the cucumbers with thinly sliced peeled beets.

Ida's
SHORE LUNCH LOAF

———»»» ❄ «««———

**MAKES SIX
SANDWICH WEDGES**

¼ cup sour cream

2 Tbsp Duchess's Mayonnaise
(page 13) or store-bought
mayonnaise

½ tsp prepared horseradish,
or to taste

¼ tsp dill seeds

One 10 in (about 1 lb) round
muffaletta loaf, focaccia, or sesame
semolina, split crosswise so it
makes a bowl with a lid

¼ cup (½ stick) unsalted butter,
divided

Fine sea salt and freshly ground
black pepper

¼ cup finely chopped Vidalia
or other sweet onion

One 10 oz package frozen
cut spinach, thawed and
squeezed dry

1 egg

8 oz smoked trout fillets

1 cup drained sliced pickled beets
(about 8 slices)

IDA HAD CERTAIN THINGS SHE TOOK WITH HER WHEN SHE WENT FISHING: A COMB, A SANDWICH OR TWO, HER FATHER'S LURES, A FLASK OF WHISKEY, AND A PINT OF WORMS FROM PENNYCUFF'S BAIT SHOP ON ANDERSON ROAD. She always swore those worms were loaded with good luck. They cost ten cents more, but she always went home with a fish or three for supper.

〜〜〜〜〜〜〜〜

HEAT YOUR OVEN TO 350°F.

MAKE A DRESSING by whisking together your sour cream, mayonnaise, horseradish, and dill seeds, then set it aside.

SCOOP OUT the inside of the bottom part of your bread loaf to make a bowl. Toast the bread that you tore from the loaf on a baking sheet until it is dry and beginning to brown, about 10 minutes. Set this bread aside to cool completely, then crush into crumbs. Melt your butter in a large skillet. Brush the inside of your bread bowl and the cut side of the top with 2 Tbsp of your melted butter and season with salt and pepper. Bake the bread cut-side up at 350°F for about 10 minutes, or until lightly browned.

HEAT YOUR SKILLET with the remaining 2 Tbsp butter over medium heat. Add the onion and cook, stirring occasionally, until tender, about 5 minutes. Squeeze the spinach one more time and add it to the onion. Cook for 3 minutes. Season with salt and pepper. Stir in ½ cup of the bread crumbs. (Reserve the rest of the bread crumbs for another use.) Let the mixture cool slightly. Stir in half of your sour cream dressing. Stir in the egg.

WHEN YOU ARE READY TO ASSEMBLE YOUR SANDWICH, spread the insides of the toasted loaf with the rest of your sour cream dressing. Place a layer of trout in the bottom of the bread bowl. Add half of your spinach mixture. Add a layer of pickled beets and top with the remaining spinach mixture. Put the top on your sandwich and press it down. Wrap the entire loaf in aluminum foil. Bake at 350°F for 20 to 25 minutes, until heated through. Unwrap your sandwich and let it cool slightly, then cut it into wedges. Serve now or allow to cool completely and tightly wrap the whole loaf or individual wedges for travel.

Gayle's
LUCKY CHICKEN POSOLE

————>>> ❄ <<<————

MAKES SOUP FOR SIX

1 Tbsp bacon grease
or olive oil

1 onion, thinly sliced

1 dried ancho chile, seeded
and thinly sliced

One 32 oz container
low-sodium chicken broth

One 28 oz can diced tomatoes,
or 2 cups fresh tomatoes,
seeded and diced

1 Tbsp seeded and minced
chipotle chile in adobo sauce,
plus more sauce to taste

One 15 oz can hominy, drained
and rinsed

2 cups shredded cooked chicken

Fine sea salt

FOR SERVING

Thinly sliced radishes

Fresh cilantro sprigs

Sliced jalapeños

Diced avocado

Thinly sliced cabbage

1 lime, cut into wedges

GAYLE FINALLY WON THE CHICKEN DROP CONTEST AT SWEET'S LOUNGE. She happened to win on the last Saturday of the month, which meant that she got to take home the money pot *and* the chicken. Gayle spent her winnings on groceries and named her new pet hen Lucky Lucy. She tosses Lucy a few of pieces of hominy every time she makes this crowd-pleasing posole.

HEAT A LARGE SOUP POT OVER MEDIUM HEAT. Add your bacon grease, onion, and ancho chile. Cook, stirring occasionally, until the onion is soft and beginning to brown, 10 to 12 minutes. Add your broth, tomatoes, chipotle in adobo, and hominy. Increase the heat and bring to a boil. Lower the heat and simmer for 15 minutes, stirring occasionally, until reduced by one-third. Stir in your chicken and simmer for 2 to 3 minutes, until the chicken is warmed through. Taste for seasonings and add more of the adobo sauce, if you like. Top each serving with a sprinkle of radishes, cilantro, jalapeños, avocado, and a tangle of cabbage and serve with lime wedges.

NOTIONS & NOTES

————◆◆◆————

ROTISSERIE CHICKEN
is perfectly fine to use in this spicy soup; a mixture of white and dark meat works best. If you want to fortify your stock, after deboning your chicken, boil the bones in the stock with an additional 2 cups water for 20 minutes. Remove the bones and strain the stock.

THIS POSOLE IS A CINCH
to put together and is a festive-looking dish to serve those last-minute dinner guests. We recommend doubling the recipe, so you can hold on to some for yourself or send a container home with friends, as it tastes even better on the second day.

WE PREFER THE LOOK OF YELLOW HOMINY,
but, of course, you can use white. Hominy is whole kernels of corn that have been treated with an alkali—like lye or slaked lime. This treatment swells the kernels and removes the hull and the germ.

Zelda's

LATE LUNCH CALDO

❖

SERVES SIX COMFORTABLY

¼ cup olive oil

1 large sweet yellow onion,
halved and thinly sliced

1 stalk celery, chopped

1 large green bell pepper,
roughly chopped

6 garlic cloves, finely chopped

¼ tsp ground allspice

½ lb tasso ham,
cut into bite-size pieces

1 lb pickled pork shoulder or
country ham (see Note), cut into
bite-size pieces

7 cups vegetable broth

One 14.5 oz can diced tomatoes
and their juices

2 cups fresh or frozen lima beans

1 lb mustard greens,
stemmed and chopped

2 bay leaves

1 Tbsp kosher salt

1 Tbsp coarsely ground black
pepper

½ lb small golden
potatoes, diced

2 medium sweet potatoes,
peeled and diced

ZELDA GOT HOME LATER THAN SHE EXPECTED—WHICH WAS FINE. The fellas from the band wouldn't even be waking up until the afternoon. She then would have their rapt attention. There wasn't a rhythm section she'd yet met that didn't fall for her caldo. Then she'd have them right where she wanted them: rested and full. After Zelda set their empty bowls in the sink, she sat at her piano and played them that tune she'd been working on for months.

IN A BIG, HEAVY-BOTTOMED POT OVER PRETTY HIGH HEAT, heat your oil until it shimmers. Add your onion, celery, and bell pepper. Cook and stir for 5 minutes, or until the onion is beginning to brown. Add the garlic and allspice and stir it all together.

ADD your tasso and pickled pork and cook and stir for 3 minutes, or until the fat begins to melt from the meats. Add your broth, scraping any browned bits up off the bottom of the pot. Add your tomatoes, lima beans, mustard greens, bay leaves, salt, and pepper. Lower the heat and simmer your caldo for 1 hour. Add your potatoes and sweet potatoes. Turn the heat up to high and bring to a boil. Lower the heat to a simmer and cook for 30 minutes, or until the potatoes are tender, stirring every now and then. Serve warm.

NOTIONS & NOTES

TASSO
is cured, smoked, highly seasoned strips of pork. The online company Cajun Grocer sells brands such as Savoie's, Poche's, and Comeaux's. Some brands make a turkey version, too.

IF YOU WANT TO PICKLE YOUR OWN MEAT, *make a brine by bringing 2 cups distilled white vinegar, 1 Tbsp yellow mustard seeds, 1 tsp celery seeds, 1 tsp Tabasco sauce, 2 bay leaves, 3 mashed garlic cloves, 2 Tbsp kosher salt, and ½ tsp cracked black pepper to a boil in a stainless-steel pot. Pour the brine into a deep container with a lid. Add 4 cups ice and stir occasionally. When the brine is absolutely cool, place 2 pounds cubed pork in the brine, making sure the meat is completely covered. Stir to remove air bubbles trapped among the cubes of pork. Cover and refrigerate for at least 3 days and up to 5. Rinse and drain before using.*

Z

PICKLED PORK,

sometimes called "pickle
meat," is made of brined pork
butt (shoulder) or loin. The
folks online at Cajun Grocer
(cajungrocer.com) can fix you
up with some of that, too.

Eliza's
SALTINE QUAIL

--->>> ❄ <<<---

SERVES FOUR

1³/₄ cups crushed saltine crackers
(about 48 crackers)

¹/₂ cup grated Parmesan cheese

¹/₃ cup Duchess's Mayonnaise
(page 13) or store-bought
mayonnaise

2 heaping Tbsp
hot honey mustard

Eight 6 to 8 oz
semiboneless quail

Kosher salt and coarsely
ground black pepper

ELIZA HAD QUITE A LARGE COLLECTION OF CERAMIC BIRDS. Each of them had a favorite food. Polly the Bluebird's was, of course, crackers. Not just any crackers, mind you. Polly had a taste for those high-dollar water crackers with sesame seeds. Eliza finally wised up to Polly's expensive taste after finding what amounted to an entire sleeve of saltines behind the china cabinet.

〰〰〰〰〰

HEAT YOUR OVEN TO 425°F. Line two large rimmed baking sheets with aluminum foil and brush generously with oil (or use baking mats). Put your cracker crumbs and cheese in a pie plate and combine them well. In a small bowl, combine your mayonnaise and mustard. Pat your quail dry and season all over with salt and pepper. Brush each quail with the mayonnaise mixture and press them one by one into the crumbs, coating all sides well. Place the quail cut-side down on the baking sheets. Bake at 425°F for 20 minutes, or until the crumbs are brown and the quail is done to your liking. We like them with the breast meat slightly pink.

NOTIONS & NOTES

◆◆◆

QUAIL IS OFTEN SOLD spatchcocked with the ribs removed and the wings and legs intact. Whole quail can also be given this crumb treatment.

YOU MAY WANT TO whip together some hot honey mustard of your own. All you need to do is mix together some yellow mustard, a dash or five of whatever hot sauce is in your cupboard, and not too much of your favorite local honey.

Edna's
SLOW-COOKED
APRICOT PORK

→≫≫ ❋ ≪←

SERVES EIGHT OR MORE

½ cup dark brown sugar

1 Tbsp hot paprika

1 Tbsp kosher salt

1 tsp ground cumin

1 tsp garlic powder

1 tsp onion powder

One 6 to 7 lb pork Boston
butt or shoulder roast

½ cup apricot jam

½ cup classic barbecue sauce
of your choice

EDNA'S BLIND DATE WASN'T ANYTHING TO WRITE HOME ABOUT, BUT HE DID AT LEAST TREAT HER TO LUNCH AT THE BEST BARBECUE RESTAURANT IN TOWN. Edna ordered the BBQ special—no pickles, extra pie. They only served her favorite buttermilk pie on Fridays, so Edna knew better than to hold back. Her date ordered baked chicken and no dessert, dealing yet another blow to his otherwise pleasant demeanor.

〜〜〜〜〜〜

IN A SMALL BOWL, COMBINE the brown sugar, paprika, salt, cumin, garlic powder, and onion powder. Coat your roast all over with the mixture. Put the roast in a slow cooker, cover, and cook on high for 8 hours. Drain the liquid from the cooker into a 4-cup glass measuring cup and allow it to settle while shredding the meat. Remove any excess fat from the meat. Remove any bones. Shred the meat and return it to the cooker.

SKIM THE FAT FROM THE RESERVED JUICES. Pour 1 cup of the juices over the meat. (Save the remaining juices for another use.) Toss your jam and barbecue sauce with the shredded meat. Cover and cook on high for 1 hour longer.

NOTIONS & NOTES

◆▬◆

**THIS SHREDDED
SLOW-COOKED PORK**
is wonderful plain or piled on squishy white sandwich buns and topped with our slaw (page 65) or in a warm corn tortilla with diced onion, plenty of fresh cilantro, and a generous squeeze of lime. Clementine's H-Town Queso (page 90) makes a great accompaniment.

THE REMAINING LIQUID
from cooking this pork roast can be used as part of the broth in Zelda's Late Lunch Caldo (page 56).

WE LOVE

the orange–chile de árbol marmalade that Stephanie McClenny makes at her Austin jam kitchen, Confituras. You might want to go ahead and try it in this recipe in place of the apricot jam, or keep it in your cupboard in case of emergency.

Pauline's
LUCKY PICKLE RELISH DOGS

➤➤➤ ❈ ⫷⫷⫷

MAKES EIGHT RELISH DOGS

PICKLE RELISH

¼ tsp brown mustard seeds

¾ cup distilled white vinegar

2 Tbsp granulated unrefined cane sugar

⅛ tsp dried dill,
or ¼ tsp chopped fresh dill

Pinch of red pepper flakes

1 English cucumber, seeded and cut into small dice (about 2 cups)

⅓ cup finely chopped red onion

⅓ cup finely chopped orange bell pepper

1 tsp cornstarch
mixed with 1 tsp water

8 top-split hot dog buns

8 skinless beef frankfurters

Store-bought yellow mustard

PAULINE COLLECTED LUCKY CHARMS. After filling five bracelets, they were starting to get in the way of her letter writing, so she began sending charms to strangers. Pauline looked for interesting names in the phone book and Sunday classifieds, then mailed off a short hello with a charm sewn to the top of a monogrammed notecard. In the ten years since she started her charm-sharing campaign, Pauline has received dozens of replies. Only once did she ever receive a charm in return.

〜〜〜〜〜〜

TO MAKE THE RELISH: Heat a small skillet over medium-high heat. Add the mustard seeds and cook until the seeds begin to pop and scoot about the skillet. Add your vinegar, sugar, dill, and red pepper flakes. Bring to a boil and let the liquid reduce by half, 5 to 8 minutes. Add your cucumber, onion, and bell pepper. Boil for 2 minutes. Stir in your cornstarch and water. Boil for 1 minute. Transfer the relish to a jar and allow it to cool completely before covering and refrigerating.

PREPARE THE HOT DOGS: Toast your buns. Butterfly your hot dogs by cutting them in half lengthwise, leaving the two sides still connected. Sear them cut-side down on a grill or griddle. Flip the dogs over and cook until heated through. Assemble your hot dogs, spooning relish down the center of each. Give each a squirt of yellow mustard and wait for the applause.

NOTIONS & NOTES
◆◆◆

**WE WASH THESE
DOGS DOWN WITH**
Rita's Roadside Attraction (page 44).

SAUSAGE AND POTATO CHIP PO'BOY WITH SLAW

MAKES FOUR SANDWICHES

1 lb Louisiana-style andouille sausage links, cut at an angle into 2 in slices

2 Tbsp vegetable oil

1 medium yellow onion, roughly chopped

2 Tbsp unbleached all-purpose flour

½ cup vegetable broth or water

1 Tbsp whole-grain Creole mustard

Four 6 in po'boy or French bread loaves, split

1 cup coleslaw (see Note)

Kettle-cooked potato chips

BEN LOVED IT WHEN HIS FAVORITE AUNT, MARY DELILAH, VISITED FROM COVINGTON. She always toted with her a full complement of his favorite brand of potato chips that she smuggled out of the factory where she was the chief quality inspector. Not a defective bag got past her. She always told Ben that he ate so many that he might one day turn into a potato chip, giving those snips and snails a run for their money. Because that's what boys are made of.

IN A BIG HOT SKILLET, sear the sausage for about 4 minutes on each side, until nicely browned. Remove the sausage from the pan. Add the oil and onion to the pan. Cook, stirring, until the onion starts to brown, 2 to 3 minutes. Stir in the flour and cook, stirring constantly, until brown as a grocery sack, about 3 minutes. Return the sausage to the pan and stir in the broth and mustard. Bring to a boil, then lower the heat to a simmer and cook for 8 to 10 minutes, until the sauce is like a gravy. Divide the smothered sausage among the bread loaves. Pile some slaw on each po'boy and stuff some chips in each.

TO MAKE A TASTY COLESLAW, COMBINE:

3 Tbsp Duchess's Mayonnaise (page 13) or store-bought mayonnaise

1 tsp light brown sugar

1 Tbsp rice vinegar

1 Tbsp buttermilk

1 tsp celery seeds

1 tsp salt

¼ tsp finely ground black pepper

⅛ tsp ground cayenne pepper

1 tsp dried dill

One 16 oz bag tricolor coleslaw blend

Afternoon

PICK-ME-UPS

NOTIONS & NOTES

◆◆◆

**WE ENJOY
SIPPING PIN CURLS**
while nibbling on Grace's
Four-Corner Nabs (page 85).

HAT TRICK GIN
from High Wire Distilling in
Charleston, South Carolina,
has botanical notes including
coriander, cardamom,
and angelica root.

Maxine's
PIN CURL

------»»» ❄ ≪≪≪------

MAKES ONE HIGHBALL

Ice cubes for the glass and shaker

1 jigger (1½ oz) gin

1 Tbsp triple sec

1 tsp lime marmalade

Splash of seltzer

Lime wedge

MAXINE STAYED IN TO TEND TO A FEW THINGS. She appreciated Rosemarie's invitation—and told her as much—but Maxine just couldn't bear the thought of attending another one of her venomous gossip sessions masquerading as cocktail hour. She made a fine and stiff drink herself, thank you, and planned on sipping one as she caught up on her house chores. Better to get something done than rub elbows with those old hens.

〜〜〜〜〜〜〜〜〜

FILL YOUR HIGHBALL GLASS and cocktail shaker with ice cubes. Put the gin, triple sec, and marmalade in your cocktail shaker. Shake for 1 whole minute. Strain into your glass and add the seltzer. Garnish with a lime wedge.

Ferdinand's
NEAT BULL SHOT

⤙⤙⤙ ❈ ⤚⤚⤚

MAKES ONE COCKTAIL

1 jigger (1½ oz) gold corn whiskey

2 jiggers (3 oz)
Bloody Mary mix

½ jigger (¾ oz)
beef consommé

2 shakes hot sauce

2 shakes bitters

Ice for the shaker

Pickled okra spear garnish

FERDINAND DECIDED TO GO FOR A SWIM. It was one of the hottest days they'd had so far this summer, and he could bear it no more. After a good cool-off in the pool, Ferdinand whipped up his favorite August cocktail, which he had to admit was a regular afternoon staple these days. He relied on it to rev up his constitution for the evening's festivities.

SHAKE the whiskey, Bloody Mary mix, consommé, hot sauce, and bitters together in your cocktail shaker with ice and strain into a teacup. Garnish with a pickled okra spear.

NOTIONS & NOTES

◆◆◆

USE THE REST OF THE CAN of beef consommé in Lenore Anne's Delta Hot Tamale Balls (page 82).

THIS DRINK IS THE PERFECT ACCOMPANIMENT to Georgia Kay's Marinated Green Bean Millefiori (page 93).

WE LIKE

the fine corn whiskey made by
Ms. Troy Ball at Troy & Sons.
Ubons Bloody Mary Mix, out
of Yazoo City, Mississippi,
is particularly nice in this
recuperative drink.

Juanita's
PEACH PUNCH BOWL

→→→ ❋ ←←←

**MAKES ABOUT
3 QUARTS OF PUNCH
AND ONE ICE RING**

ICE RING

5 cups purified water

8 whole star anise pods

8 thin rounds unpeeled
fresh ginger

2 fresh peaches, peeled,
pitted, and sliced

1 lemon, halved and thinly sliced

PUNCH

2 peach herbal tea bags

$\frac{1}{2}$ cup granulated unrefined
cane sugar

$\frac{1}{2}$ cup freshly squeezed
lemon juice

1 cup peach brandy

$3\frac{1}{2}$ cups (28 oz) ginger ale, chilled

One 750 ml bottle prosecco,
chilled

JUANITA ALWAYS PUT FRESH PEACHES IN HER GINGER ALE. It was a habit she learned from her neighbor, Marilyn, who always used them to garnish their afternoon cocktails whenever Juanita would visit. Only later did she find out that soft-spoken Marilyn collected the pits to crush into smithereens and use as filling for her handmade dolls.

〜〜〜〜〜〜〜〜〜

TO MAKE THE ICE RING: At least 24 hours before you are going to serve your punch, clear a spot in your freezer for the ice ring to set. Boil your purified water and allow it to cool completely. Arrange the star anise pods in a 5-cup ring mold or shape of your choice. Scatter the ginger, peaches, and lemon slices around the bottom of the mold. Pour 1 cup of the cooled water over the fruit and place the ring in the freezer until solid. Add the rest of the water. Freeze the ring solid.

TO MAKE THE PUNCH: Bring 1 cup water to a boil in a small pot and add your tea bags. Remove from the heat and let the tea steep for 5 minutes. Remove the tea bags and add the sugar, stirring until dissolved. Stir in your lemon juice and brandy. Chill thoroughly.

WHEN READY TO SERVE, pour the tea mixture into your punch bowl.

DIP the bottom of the ice ring mold in hot water briefly to loosen the ice. Place a sheet pan over the ice and then invert it. Add the ice ring to the punch bowl, fruit-side up. (Doing this prior to adding the ginger ale to the punch cuts down on splashing.) Add your ginger ale and prosecco. Stir gently, then ladle into punch cups and serve.

Louise's
SARDINE CRISPS

>>> ❄ <<<

**MAKES ABOUT
EIGHTEEN CRISPS**

3 Tbsp Dijon mustard

2 Tbsp unsalted butter,
at room temperature

One 17.3 oz package frozen
puff pastry sheets

Two 3.75 oz tins boneless, skinless
sardines in tomato sauce, drained

1 egg, beaten with
1 Tbsp water

Flaky sea salt

LOUISE KEPT HER FAVORITE EARRINGS HIDDEN IN A SARDINE CAN IN THE CUPBOARD. They weren't worth more than a dime, but she thought it was a fine hiding place for something that held such sentimental value. Louise didn't even wear them that often, for fear they might break as soon as she held them up to her ears. But she would get them out every once in a while, just to pay them a visit and recall the details of that too-short summer she spent on the coast.

LINE two baking sheets with parchment paper, aluminum foil, or baking mats and set aside.

IN A SMALL BOWL, mix together your mustard and room-temperature butter. Roll each of your pastry sheets into a very thin 14-inch square. Spread the dough with the mustard-butter mixture. Break the sardines into small pieces and scatter them over the dough. Roll each square of dough up into a log. Cut into rounds ¼ inch thick and place them about 1 inch apart on the baking sheets. Brush the tops with the beaten egg mixture and sprinkle with flaky salt. Chill the rounds for about 10 minutes in the freezer.

PREHEAT your oven to 425°F.

BAKE the rounds for 12 to 15 minutes, until deep brown and crisp. Serve hot.

NOTIONS & NOTES

◆◆◆

ANCHOVIES AND OTHER TINNED FISH ARE GOOD IN THESE AS WELL.

YOU CAN RESERVE THE OIL
from the sardines to use in a Caesar-style dressing on a salad or drizzled over pasta.

TRY ADDING SOME OF THE SARDINE OIL
to your butter for a bagna cauda–type flavor in Agnes's Graton Firecracker Popcorn (page 78).

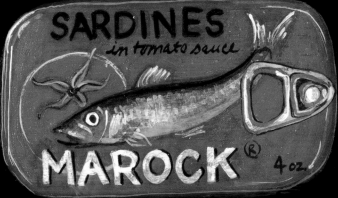

SARDINES
in tomato sauce
MAROCK ®
4 oz.

Clara's
OYSTER SHOT

>>> ❄ <<<

SERVES TWO

¼ small baby fennel bulb,
very finely chopped
(about 1 Tbsp), plus
1 Tbsp chopped fronds

½ small shallot, very finely
chopped (about 1 Tbsp)

½ cup Champagne vinegar

½ tsp coarsely ground
pink peppercorns

Fine sea salt (if needed, see Note)

Splash of sparkling rosé, if desired

1 dozen freshly shucked oysters
on the half shell, chilled

ONCE CLARA AND BEN WERE IN NEW ORLEANS, THEY TRIED EVERYTHING.
It was their anniversary, after all, and Clara's great-grandmother made
a point of telling Ben that the proper gift was a string of pearls. Pearls
or no, this was their first time back in the Crescent City since their
honeymoon, and they were bound and determined to make it count.

IN A SMALL GLASS BOWL, mix together your fennel, shallot, vinegar, pink peppercorns,
and salt (if you're going to need it). Chill until nice and cold, but not frozen. Add a
splash of sparkling wine (if using). Spoon just a tiny bit of sauce over each oyster and
add a sprinkle of fennel fronds as you eat them.

NOTIONS & NOTES

◆◆◆

EAT ONE OF YOUR OYSTERS
without any of the mignonette
sauce on it. See how briny they
taste and use that to determine
how much salt, if any, is needed.
And if you happen to be serving
a sparkling wine with the oysters,
go ahead and pour a big splash
into the sauce to give it a little
effervescence.

Agnes's
GRATON FIRECRACKER POPCORN

—————— ❄ ——————

SERVES FOUR FOR SNACKING

2 Tbsp salted butter

½ tsp Cajun seasoning

2 Tbsp canola oil

¼ cup popcorn kernels

One 2 oz bag puffy fried pork rinds, crushed

One 1.75 oz bag spicy dry-roasted peanuts

IT HAD BEEN YEARS SINCE UNCLE PRID DIED, BUT AGNES STILL MISSED THEIR SUMMER SUPPERS OUT ON THE FRONT LAWN. He always kept treats on hand to give to the neighbor kids who happened by on those evenings. One year, the Jones boys asked him if he had any bang snaps left over from the Fourth. Uncle Prid promised them he'd have some the next time, but that time never came. Agnes kept a box of firecrackers under her bed, just in case.

IN A SMALL SAUCEPAN OVER LOW HEAT, melt your butter with the Cajun seasoning and set it aside. Heat a large pot (about 5 quarts) with a lid over medium-high heat. Add your oil and 3 kernels of popcorn. Set the lid ajar. When you hear the corn pop, add the rest of the corn and cover the pot. When you hear the first few popping sounds, begin shaking the pot vigorously while holding the lid slightly ajar to let out steam. When popping subsides, sprinkle in your butter. Toss the pork rinds with the popcorn. Sprinkle in the peanuts.

NOTIONS & NOTES

——— ◆◆◆ ———

YOU CAN PUFF YOUR OWN PORK rinds in the microwave using Carolina Gold Nuggets Microwave Pork Puffies, found online.

The Suzy B's

SPINACH AND MUSHROOM FRITO PIE

→→→ ❄ ←←←

MAKES SIX SERVINGS

1²/₃ cups half-and-half, divided

2¹/₂ tsp cornstarch

1 tsp finely ground
white pepper

¹/₂ tsp fine sea salt

¹/₂ tsp ancho chile powder

Dash of cayenne pepper

Dash of grated nutmeg

2 Tbsp unsalted butter

4 garlic cloves, finely chopped

¹/₂ cup roughly chopped
white onion

8 oz white button
mushrooms, roughly chopped

1 large jalapeño,
seeded and diced

Two 10 oz packages frozen
chopped spinach, thawed and
squeezed dry

2 cups (8 oz) grated pepper Jack
cheese, divided

One 9.5 oz bag or six individual
1 oz bags corn chips

Chopped fresh cilantro

FRANNY ALWAYS GREETED HER GUESTS WITH AN ENTHUSIASTIC *"HOW YA DURIN'?"* On this night, everyone was celebrating the launch of the Ward family's latest addition to their shrimping fleet, *The Suzy B*. Glasses overflowed with Champagne, and Franny was committed to serving her favorite food. After the party, Mrs. Coleman sent her a hefty dry-cleaning bill, and Franny refused to give her another reason to complain.

〰〰〰〰〰〰〰〰〰

IN A LITTLE BOWL, mix 2 Tbsp of the half-and-half with the cornstarch and set it aside. In a small saucepan over medium heat, bring the remaining half-and-half, the white pepper, salt, chile powder, cayenne, and nutmeg to a simmer. Give the cornstarch mixture a stir and add it to the saucepan, stirring continuously. Bring to a full boil and cook, stirring, for 1 minute. Remove from the heat and set aside.

HEAT a large deep skillet with a lid over medium-high heat and melt the butter. Add the garlic, onion, mushrooms, and jalapeño. Cover and cook for 5 minutes. Add the spinach. Stir in 1 cup of your cheese and the half-and-half mixture.

NOTIONS & NOTES

◆◆◆

IF SO INCLINED, serve each guest's pie in a Frito bag. Do this by transferring each portion into a snack bag that has been split down the center.

WHEN YOU ARE READY TO MAKE YOUR FRITO PIES, line a rimmed baking sheet with aluminum foil and arrange six servings of corn chips in flattened mounds on the foil. Position an oven rack in the upper middle position of your oven and heat your broiler.

SPOON about ¹/₂ cup of the spinach mixture over each mound of chips and top with the remaining 1 cup cheese. Broil for 6 to 8 minutes, until all bubbly and warmed through. Move each mound to a plate for serving. Garnish with cilantro.

Lenore Anne's
DELTA HOT TAMALE BALLS

⊱⟩⟩⟩ ❋ ⟨⟨⟨⊰

**MAKES ABOUT
TEN DOZEN MEATBALLS**

1 tsp red pepper flakes

1 tsp dried oregano

1 tsp ground cumin

1 tsp ground coriander

2 tsp kosher salt

1 Tbsp chili powder

1 Tbsp olive oil

1 medium white onion,
finely chopped, divided

1 poblano pepper, seeded
and diced, divided

3 garlic cloves, finely chopped

One 6 oz can tomato paste

$1/2$ tsp granulated unrefined cane
sugar

$5^3/_4$ cups (46 oz)
tomato juice, divided

One 10.5 oz can beef consommé,
or $1^1/_3$ cups beef stock

2 bay leaves

1 lb ground sirloin

1 lb hot pork breakfast sausage

$1^1/_2$ cups masa harina or cornmeal

$1/4$ cup unbleached
all-purpose flour

**LENORE ANNE CARRIED AT LEAST THREE BAGS OF EMPTY TUPPERWARE
CONTAINERS WITH HER EVERY TIME SHE VISITED JOE'S WHITE FRONT
CAFE IN ROSEDALE.** Miss Barbara had her spoiled. She'd make Lenore
Anne's special order, if she called at least two weeks ahead. But today,
Lenore Anne was caught without any Delta hot tamales in her freezer,
so she had to make do for another of Ginny's baby showers. Lenore Anne
never threw a party without tamales on her table.

〰〰〰〰〰〰〰〰〰〰〰〰〰〰〰

IN A SMALL BOWL, make a spice blend with your red
pepper flakes, oregano, cumin, coriander, salt, and
chili powder.

HEAT a large heavy-bottomed pot with a lid over
medium heat. Add the oil. When the oil starts to
shimmer, add half of your onion and half of your
poblano. Cook and stir for 2 minutes. Add the
garlic, tomato paste, and sugar. Add half of your
spice blend. Cook and stir for 1 minute. Add 5 cups
of your tomato juice, the consommé, and bay leaves.
Increase the heat to high and bring to a boil. Lower
the heat to a simmer and let the sauce cook as you
make the tamale balls.

NOTIONS & NOTES

◈◈◈

YOU CAN USE YOUR
favorite taco seasoning mix
in place of or in addition to
the spice blend in this
meatball recipe.

IN A BIG BOWL, using your hands, combine the sirloin, sausage, remaining ¾ cup
tomato juice, and remaining onion and poblano. Work in the masa harina, flour, and
your remaining spice blend. Form heaping tablespoon-size meatballs. Drop the meatballs into the simmering sauce and put the lid on your pot, slightly ajar. Cook over low
heat for 2 hours.

●━━━   ━━━

IF THIS RECIPE

just gives you a craving for tamales, we recommend ordering some online from the Texas
Tamale Company or Scott's Hot Tamales in Greenville, Mississippi. If and when you have a wild
hair, take a drive through the Mississippi Delta where you will find a particular style of tamale
that took root in this part of the South more than a century ago. Make sure to visit Joe's White
Front Cafe on Main Street in Rosedale. Don't forget, it's BYOT (Bring Your Own Tupperware).

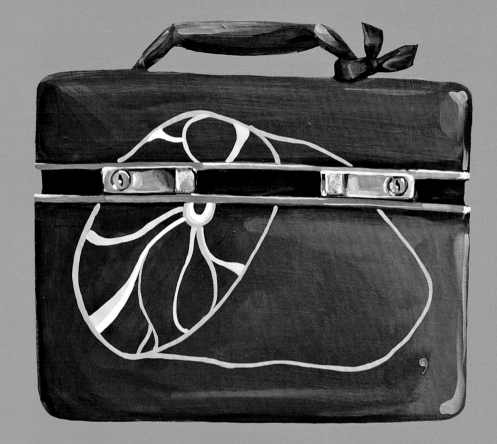

Grace's
FOUR-CORNER NABS

>>> ❋ <<<

**MAKES ABOUT TWENTY-FOUR
SANDWICH CRACKERS**

CRACKERS

1 tsp malt syrup

1/2 cup warm water, heated to 110°F

1 tsp instant yeast

1 1/2 cups unbleached bread flour

1/2 tsp ground turmeric

1/2 tsp kosher salt

1/2 tsp baking powder

1 Tbsp Cheddar cheese powder,
if desired

1 cup (4 oz) finely grated
extra-sharp Cheddar cheese

1/4 cup cold shortening or lard

1 egg, beaten with 1 tsp water
and a pinch of salt

Flaky salt to sprinkle on crackers

FILLING

1 cup chunky peanut butter

2 Tbsp powdered sugar

2 tsp kosher salt

Pinch of cayenne pepper

GRACE COULDN'T TAKE ANY CHANCES, SO SHE FIT ALL SORTS OF CONTIN-GENCIES INTO HER TRAIN CASE. This was, after all, the first time she was making the trip to visit her granddaughter all the way over in Texas. For all Grace knew, they ate brisket for breakfast, lunch, and dinner. That just wouldn't do. No, ma'am. Grace made sure that they would have some proper Alabama staples within reach during her visit. She packed some Nabs at the last minute, just to make the trip bearable.

TO MAKE THE CRACKERS: In a small bowl, stir the malt syrup into your warm water. Sprinkle the yeast over that syrup mixture and let it sit for 5 minutes, or until it's a little bit foamy. In a food processor with the blade attachment, combine the flour, turmeric, kosher salt, baking powder, and that cheese powder (if using) and pulse. Add the grated cheese and pulse several times to combine. Remove the lid and scatter in small pieces of the shortening. Replace the lid and pulse again. With the processor running, add the yeast mixture and blend until a tight dough is formed, about 1 minute. Form the dough into a 1/4-inch-thick slab and wrap it in food wrap. Set the dough in a warm place to proof for 1 hour.

ROLL YOUR DOUGH out into an 18-by-7-inch rectangle. Fold the dough in thirds like a business letter. Turn the folded side toward you, roll out again, and then fold just as before. Cover the dough in food wrap and refrigerate for 1 hour.

PLACE THE DOUGH'S folded edge in front of you and cut the dough in half, making two pieces about 9 by 3 1/2 inches. Return half of the dough to the refrigerator.

Continued

PUT A BAKING SHEET–SIZE PIECE OF PARCHMENT PAPER on your counter. Cut your dough in half from folded side to folded side, making two pieces about 4½ inches wide. Using a pasta machine, roll the dough down to the #3 setting, or roll out until very, very thin with a rolling pin to a rectangle of about 15 by 5 inches. Place your dough on the parchment paper. Using a scalloped rolling cutter or a pizza cutter, cut out 2½-inch squares. Slip the paper with the dough squares onto a baking sheet. Repeat with the rest of the dough.

LET THE CRACKERS REST and rise for 1 hour.

HEAT YOUR OVEN TO 350°F. Dock each cracker several times with the tines of a fork to keep them from getting too puffy. Brush the crackers with the beaten egg mixture. Sprinkle with flaky salt. Bake for 15 to 17 minutes, until shiny and crisp. Remove your crackers to a wire rack to cool while you make your filling.

TO MAKE THE FILLING: In a food processor, blend the peanut butter, powdered sugar, salt, and cayenne together.

WHEN THE CRACKERS ARE COOL, spread a thin layer of the peanut butter filling on the unsalted side of one cracker and top with another cracker, salt-side up. Repeat to fill all the crackers.

NOTIONS & NOTES

THESE CRACKERS AND FILLING
can also be served chip-and-dip style along
with fresh apple slices and celery sticks.

**IF YOU DON'T HAVE A DECORATIVE
PASTRY CUTTER ON HAND,**
try using a rotary fabric cutter with a scallop
blade. Just be sure to clean it thoroughly
before returning it to your sewing box.

THE FILLING RECIPE IS ALSO
awfully close to that of peanut marzipan,
which you can make yourself by adding
more powdered sugar to create a sturdier,
shape-able "dough," or just look for the
de la Rosa brand at your local Latino
grocery. They are sometimes sold as
individually wrapped candies, but you can
also find them packaged by the pound
in a particularly gorgeous yellow box that
features a giant red rose.

Joseph's

SALMON SPREAD

——— ⟫⟫⟫ ❄ ⟪⟪⟪ ———

SERVES SIX TO EIGHT

One 7.5 oz can wild-caught, fancy-grade red salmon, drained, skin and bones removed

1 hard-boiled or steamed egg (see page 50), white and yolk separated

1 Tbsp finely chopped red onion

1 Tbsp capers

1 Tbsp freshly squeezed lemon juice

2 tsp Lea & Perrins Marinade for Chicken with White Wine and Herbs

One 8 oz package cream cheese, at room temperature

Toast points for serving

MARY WASN'T A TRADITIONAL BEAUTY BY ANY MEANS, BUT HER PLAINNESS BELIED A RAUCOUS PERSONALITY THAT ALL THE FRANKLIN COUNTY BOYS ADORED. Joseph was especially fond of Mary's quick wit and quirky habits, like her weekly routine of typing up words of wisdom onto little slivers of found paper and tucking them in between the pages of random books at the Goodwill. She inspired Joseph to send a love note for his bay beauty down Apalachicola way. Which he packed in a salmon can, along with a collection of bluebird feathers that he had been collecting for her while they were apart.

〜〜〜〜〜〜〜〜〜〜〜〜〜

FLAKE YOUR SALMON into small pieces in a medium bowl. Crumble in your egg yolk and add the onion and capers. Stir in your lemon juice and Lea & Perrins. Using the large-hole side of a box grater, grate the egg white into the salmon. Add the cream cheese and stir until blended. Serve with toast points.

NOTIONS & NOTES

——— ◆◆◆ ———

IF YOU ARE FEELING EXTRA FANCY, spray a 2-cup mold or bowl with cooking oil. Line the mold with food wrap. Place capers or other pickled vegetables in a mosaic pattern in the bottom of the mold. Fill it with your salmon spread and chill for 1 hour. Invert the mold onto a serving plate and remove the food wrap.

Clementine's
CRAWFISH PUPPIES DIPPED IN H-TOWN QUESO

⟶⟶ ❋ ⟵⟵

MAKES FOUR SERVINGS

CLEMENTINE PRAYED OVER THE QUESO, JUST AS HER GRANDMOTHER ALWAYS HAD BEFORE HER. Abuelita believed that the garnet-red oil that pooled on top held secrets from the past and promises for the future. As a child, Clementine did not put too much faith in the ritual. But, ever since her prayers were answered, she believed that queso was a direct line to her beloved *abuelita*.

CHEESE DIP

1/4 cup vegetable oil

1/4 cup finely chopped yellow onion

3/4 cup diced tomatoes

1/2 tsp finely chopped garlic

1 tsp chili powder

1 tsp hot paprika

1/4 tsp kosher salt

1/4 cup unbleached all-purpose flour

2 cups (8 oz) shredded American cheese

CRAWFISH PUPPIES

Vegetable oil for deep-frying

3/4 cup self-rising cornmeal

3/4 cup self-rising flour

1 tsp light brown sugar

1 tsp fine sea salt

1 tsp baking soda

1/2 cup buttermilk

1/4 cup beer

1 large egg

1/2 lb fresh or frozen domestic crawfish tail meat with fat

TO MAKE THE CHEESE DIP: In a medium saucepan, heat your oil over low heat. Add your onion, tomatoes, garlic, chili powder, paprika, and salt. Cook, stirring occasionally, for 6 to 8 minutes, until the tomatoes are very broken down. Whisk together your all-purpose flour and 1/4 cup water to make a paste, then whisk it into the tomato mixture. Raise the heat to medium and bring to a boil for 1 full minute. Whisking constantly, add the cheese a little at a time and continue to cook and stir until the cheese is melted. Keep warm.

TO MAKE THE CRAWFISH PUPPIES: Heat at least 2 inches of oil in a deep, heavy-bottomed pot over medium heat or deep fryer to 350°F.

IN A LARGE BOWL, combine all the remaining ingredients together to make a thick batter. Drop the batter by the tablespoon into your hot oil. Fry, stirring with a slotted spoon, for 2 minutes, or until the puppies are deep brown and crisp. Serve hot with the cheese dip.

NOTIONS & NOTES

THIS PARTICULAR STYLE of cheese dip is inspired by the queso from the old Felix Mexican Restaurant in Houston, Texas—a beloved Tex-Mex spot that was opened by Felix Tijerina in 1937 and fed Houstonians at multiple locations for more than seven decades. The last remaining Felix location closed in 2008, but you can still get "Felix's World Famous Queso" at El Patio Restaurant, also in Houston.

LISA FAIN, THE HOMESICK TEXAN, perfected her own version of the Felix queso. Her books and blog are wonderful sources for all things Tex-Mex.

Georgia Kay's

MARINATED GREEN BEAN MILLEFIORI

MAKES FOUR DOZEN

1 lb fresh haricots verts or tender green beans, blanched (see Note)

1½ cups vegetable marinade (see Note) or your favorite vinaigrette

1 loaf white sandwich bread, sliced, crusts removed

¼ cup Durkee's Famous Sauce

¼ cup Duchess's Mayonnaise (page 13)

4 oz cream cheese, at room temperature

GEORGIA KAY ALWAYS LOOKED FORWARD TO SNAPPING BEANS. It seemed the only time she had to herself anymore. This year, she doubled her usual planting of pole beans, just so she could spend the fall snapping and canning. She knew she set herself up for more work, but it'd be worth it. Now all Georgia Kay had to do was make it through the rest of summer.

〜〜〜〜〜〜〜〜

PUT YOUR GREEN BEANS in a resealable bag with your marinade and refrigerate for at least 2 hours and up to 24 hours.

WHEN READY TO MAKE YOUR ROLL-UPS, roll each slice of bread flat with a rolling pin. In a small bowl, make a spread with your Durkee's sauce, mayonnaise, and cream cheese. Give each slice of bread a thin coat of the spread. Place 3 green beans in a stack near one edge of the bread and roll the bread around the beans tightly, making a cylinder filled with beans. Place the rolls, seam-side down, on a baking sheet. Cover with food wrap and refrigerate for at least 2 hours or overnight. When ready to serve, cut each roll crosswise into four pieces.

· ·

TO BLANCH GREEN BEANS: *Bring 1 gallon of water to a boil with ½ tsp baking soda. Fill a large bowl with ice water. Drop the beans into the boiling water and let them cook for 3 minutes. Drain the beans in a colander. Plunge the colander into the ice water. Drain the beans when cool.*

NOTIONS & NOTES

◆ ◆ ◆

THIS IS A GREAT MARINADE FOR ALL SORTS OF VEGETABLES:

1 cup soybean oil

¼ cup white wine vinegar

2 Tbsp red wine vinegar

½ tsp honey

½ tsp Dijon mustard

2 garlic cloves, very finely chopped

2 Tbsp finely chopped shallot

2 Tbsp very finely chopped red bell pepper

½ tsp fine sea salt

¼ tsp dried marjoram

Pinch of red pepper flakes

Freshly ground black pepper

Put everything in a jar with a tight-fitting lid and shake until well combined.

Dinner Dates

+ LATE-NIGHT TAKES

Angela's
PISSALADIÈRE
⟶≫ ❄ ≪⟵

MAKES ONE PIQUANT TART

1 Tbsp unsalted butter

1 Tbsp extra-virgin olive oil

1 large sweet yellow onion,
halved and thinly sliced

4 sprigs fresh thyme

1 tsp white wine vinegar

$1/4$ tsp finely ground
white pepper

$1/4$ tsp kosher salt

One $9^{1}/_{2}$ by 11 in
sheet frozen puff pastry
(half of a 17.3 oz package), thawed

$1/4$ cup Niçoise olives,
pitted and chopped

One 2 oz can anchovy fillets
packed in oil, drained
and blotted dry

ANGELA RAN A BATH, LIT A CIGARETTE, AND READ SOME POETRY. A night-time getaway was what she needed. With the right ambiance she could remove herself and harken back to the semester she spent in Paris. That was when it had all changed. Candlelight, the scent of savory pastry baking, and measured words transported her as she soaked.

IN A MEDIUM SKILLET OVER MEDIUM HEAT, melt your butter with the oil. Brush a rimmed baking sheet with a little of the butter mixture and set it aside. To your skillet, add the onion, thyme, vinegar, white pepper, and salt. When the mixture begins to simmer, turn the heat to low and cook, stirring occasionally, for 25 minutes, or until the onions are deeply caramelized. Remove the thyme stems.

HEAT YOUR OVEN TO 450°F.

PLACE THE PUFF PASTRY SHEET ON THE BAKING SHEET. Brush a $1/2$-inch border of water around the edge of the dough. Fold a $1/2$-inch border around the edges, forming a picture frame. Using a fork, make several punctures in the dough across the center of the frame. Spread your caramelized onions over the surface of the interior of the frame. Sprinkle your olives over the onions. Place the anchovies in a lattice pattern over the onions. Bake at 450°F for 20 minutes, or until the dough is puffed and a deep golden brown. Cool for 5 minutes, then cut into pieces and serve.

NOTIONS & NOTES

USE THE SECOND SHEET
of dough to make Louise's
Sardine Crisps (page 74).

Esther's
DIMINUTIVE CRISP CORN AND CURRY COMEBACK

————— ✺ —————

MAKES SNACKS FOR FOUR

CURRY COMEBACK

1 cup plain yogurt

1 Tbsp red chili sauce

2 Tbsp very finely chopped white onion

1 tsp curry powder

1 tsp Kashmiri chile powder

1/4 tsp fine sea salt

CORN

1/2 lb fresh baby corn, blanched, or two 15 oz cans baby corn, drained and rinsed

1 tsp mashed garlic

1 tsp very, very finely chopped fresh ginger

1/2 tsp Kashmiri chile powder

1/4 tsp fine sea salt

Vegetable oil for frying

1/2 cup cornstarch

1/2 cup unbleached all-purpose flour

1 cup cold seltzer

NOTIONS & NOTES

————— ◆ —————

THIS CURRY comeback sauce is great with sweet potato chips.

IF YOU NEED TO, substitute sweet paprika with a pinch of cayenne for the Kashmiri chile powder.

ESTHER HAD A MIDNIGHT SNACK. She felt compelled to stay up and pick apart the night's conversation. A can of baby corn was all she could find, and it had been on the shelf for a while. Esther had held on to it because her mother loved seeing it in her green salad, along with a generous dollop of comeback dressing. She'd make do—and she'd try to work through her frustration by morning.

～～～～～～～～

TO MAKE THE CURRY COMEBACK: In a bowl, mix all the ingredients together and let the sauce hang out while you make the corn.

TO MAKE THE CORN: Set a paper grocery bag inside a rimmed baking sheet and set aside until it is time to fry. Put your corn in a large bowl and toss it with the garlic, ginger, chile powder, and salt. Heat at least 2 inches of oil in a deep, heavy-bottomed skillet over medium heat to 350°F.

MAKE A BATTER by combining your cornstarch, flour, and seltzer. Pour the batter over the corn and toss it to coat.

RIGHT BEFORE FRYING EACH BATCH, toss the corn around again so that it is evenly coated. Fry the corn a few at a time, turning as needed, until crisp and golden all over, 5 to 8 minutes. Remove from the oil and set on the paper grocery sack to drain the excess oil. Serve immediately with your curry comeback for dipping.

Fanny's
OXTAIL AND RED ONION SOUP GRATINÉ

✧ ➤❄◆❄◀ ✧

MAKES SOUP FOR FOUR

2 lb oxtails

2 Tbsp unbleached
all-purpose flour, divided

1 1/2 tsp finely ground
black pepper

2 Tbsp olive oil

6 cups thinly sliced red onion

3 bay leaves

3 large sprigs fresh thyme

2 Tbsp
Worcestershire sauce

6 cups beef bone broth or stock

4 thick slices hearty white bread or
baguette, toasted

1 cup (4 oz) grated aged Swiss or
Gruyère cheese

FANNY KEPT SUNGLASSES AND A HANDKERCHIEF IN HER APRON POCKET.
She was teary-prone anyway, and today's news, coupled with the onions—whew, she was a faucet. Even so, she tried her best to pull herself together, taking care to make perfect paper-thin slices, just as her grandmother taught her.

SPRINKLE your oxtails with 1 Tbsp of the flour and season with the pepper.

HEAT A BIG DUTCH OVEN over medium heat. Add the oil and heat until it starts to shimmy. Add your oxtails and cook for 6 to 8 minutes, until browned, turning and cooking on all sides. Set your oxtails aside. Add the onion, bay leaves, and thyme to the pot and cook and stir for 2 minutes. Sprinkle the remaining 1 Tbsp flour over the onions and cook and stir for 2 minutes. Stir in your Worcestershire sauce and broth. Return your oxtails to the pot. Increase the heat to high and bring to a boil. Lower the heat and simmer, with the lid of the pot slightly ajar, for 2 hours, or until your oxtails are falling to pieces. If desired, skim the fat from the surface of the soup.

POSITION YOUR OVEN RACKS so the Dutch oven will fit beneath your broiler and heat the broiler. Remove the lid of the pot. Nestle the bread slices into the oxtails and sprinkle them with the cheese. Broil for 2 minutes, or until the cheese is lightly browned and bubbling. Serve at once.

NOTIONS & NOTES
➤◆◆◆◀

IF YOU WOULD LIKE
to eat a little neater at the table, shred the meat from the oxtail and return it to the pot before adding your bread. Set the bones aside to gnaw on in the privacy of your own kitchen.

Ula Mae's
SPOONBREAD WITH OYSTERS AND ARTICHOKES

ULA MAE WAS JOTTING DOWN IDEAS FOR WHAT TO SERVE AT SUNDAY'S SPECIAL-OCCASION BRUNCH. Things that go with oysters: cornmeal. Perfect, she thought. Johnny could set out on his oyster skiff a time or two before everyone got to town. And Big Daddy was bringing his fryer, so supper was taken care of.

SPOONBREAD

6 Tbsp unsalted butter, cut into pieces

1½ cups corn flour (we like Zatarain's Wonderful Fish Fri seafood breading)

2 tsp fine sea salt

2 cups water, ready at a boil

2 cups whole milk

4 large or jumbo eggs, very well beaten

2 tsp baking powder

OYSTERS

1 pt (about 24) shucked oysters, drained, liquor reserved (two 12 oz containers)

4 Tbsp (½ stick) unsalted butter

1 large sprig fresh thyme

1 shallot, finely chopped

1 Tbsp finely chopped garlic

1 Tbsp unbleached all-purpose flour

¼ cup chopped fresh flat-leaf parsley

½ tsp red pepper flakes

½ lemon, zested and juiced

One 9 oz package frozen artichoke hearts or fresh artichoke hearts

THESE STEWED oysters are also quite good served with rice grits (see page 34).

TO MAKE THE SPOONBREAD: Heat your oven to 350°F. Put your butter in a large, deep (11 cups or 9 by 7 by 2½ inches) baking dish or casserole dish and place it in the oven as it heats.

IN A LARGE BOWL, whisk together your corn flour and salt. Pour the boiling water over the corn flour and give it a thorough whisking. Take your baking dish from the oven and whisk most of the butter into the corn flour. Add the milk and whisk to combine. Whisk in your beaten eggs and baking powder. Pour this into the dish and bake for 40 to 45 minutes, until puffy and deep golden on top. While this is baking, ready your oysters.

TO MAKE THE OYSTERS: Add enough water to the reserved oyster liquor to make 1½ cups. Heat a medium skillet over medium-high heat. When your skillet is hot, add the butter and swirl it around the pan until melted. Add the thyme and oysters. Cook just until the oysters begin to plump up and ruffle around the edges. With a slotted spoon, move the oysters to a bowl and set aside.

TO YOUR SKILLET, add the shallot and garlic. Cook and stir for 2 minutes. Stir in the flour and cook and stir for 2 minutes. Stir in your reserved oyster liquor, parsley, red pepper flakes, lemon zest, and lemon juice. Add your artichoke hearts. Cook, stirring occasionally, for 2 to 3 minutes, until the sauce is slightly thickened and shiny. Gently stir in the oysters and any accumulated liquor.

TO SERVE, spoon oysters over each portion of spoonbread.

NOTIONS & NOTES

LOOK FOR OYSTERS
that are sized "select." This means there are 20 to 30 medium oysters per pint. If you like your oysters on the smaller side, ask for "standard." If you like larger oysters, what we call "saddlebags," look for big ones deemed "counts" that have 20 or fewer oysters per pint.

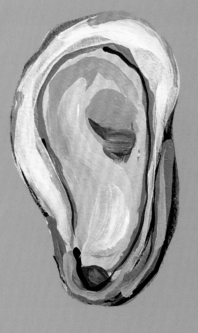

9

MIRACLE

NONE

CORN MEAL

BETTER

MIRACLE FEED MILLS

Stella's
HARISSA GOLD CHICKEN

————————— ✴ —————————

MAKES DINNER FOR FOUR

3 Tbsp mild or
hot harissa paste

$1/2$ tsp ground cumin

3 Tbsp extra-virgin
olive oil

$3/4$ lb very small golden potatoes,
larger ones cut in half

$1/2$ lb golden carrots, peeled and cut
into 2 in chunks

2 cups fresh or frozen peeled pearl
onions (one 8 oz package fresh or
half of a 14 oz package frozen)

$1/2$ cup roughly chopped
yellow bell pepper

4 chicken leg quarters

$1/3$ cup chopped golden
sultana raisins

1 lemon

$1/2$ cup plain yogurt

1 garlic clove, finely chopped

Kosher salt and freshly ground
black pepper

$1/4$ cup chopped fresh mint leaves

$1/4$ cup chopped fresh flat-leaf
parsley

2 Tbsp chopped fresh dill

STELLA HAD AN ENTIRE ROOM FILLED WITH GOLD OBJECTS THAT SHE HAD COLLECTED OVER THE YEARS. One day, she decided to send them all off to friends. She packed up the brass four-leaf clover for Maureen. Stella knew she just had to give the gold-painted pulley bone to Cordelia. And the can of harissa that she brought home from Memphis was bound for Gina's mailbox. Stella could hardly contain her excitement as she marked her wall calendar with the exact dates upon which each friend would receive her package.

〰〰〰〰〰〰〰〰〰〰〰〰〰〰〰〰〰〰〰〰〰

HEAT YOUR OVEN TO 425°F.

IN A SMALL BOWL, whisk together the harissa, cumin, and oil. In a large bowl, combine the potatoes, carrots, onions, and bell pepper. Toss the vegetables with half of your harissa mixture. Place the vegetables in the center of a large rimmed baking sheet.

ADD THE CHICKEN to the bowl and coat it with the remaining harissa mixture. Arrange the chicken skin-side up with the thighs facing out in each corner of the baking sheet. Bake at 425°F for 20 minutes. Add your raisins. Zest your lemon over the chicken and vegetables. Continue to bake for 20 to 25 minutes more, until the chicken is crispy golden and a thermometer registers 165°F at the thickest part of the thigh. Spoon any accumulated juices over the chicken.

IN A SMALL BOWL, stir together your yogurt, garlic, and the juice from your lemon. Season with salt and pepper. Drizzle the yogurt sauce over the chicken and sprinkle with the mint, parsley, and dill.

NOTIONS & NOTES

——— ◆◆ ———

WE LIKE TO SERVE THIS
Tunisian-inspired dish spooned over couscous.

HARISSA IS A NORTH AFRICAN SAUCE
made from a paste that includes smoked hot chiles, garlic, olive oil, and spices like cumin, coriander, caraway, and mint and sometimes dried tomatoes.

SHERRY POT PIE

MAKES THREE
INDIVIDUAL PIES

FILLING

2 cups cooked, diced chicken
meat cut into small pieces

One 10 oz bag frozen mixed
vegetables, thawed

One 10.5 oz can cream of chicken
and mushroom soup

$1/3$ cup whole milk

1 Tbsp sherry,
or to your liking

$1/4$ tsp coarsely ground black
pepper

CRUSTS

One 8 oz box "Jiffy"
Buttermilk Biscuit Mix

$1/2$ cup cold water

1 egg, beaten
with 1 tsp water

IT WAS A TUESDAY NIGHT, AND THE CORNER GROCERY WAS ALL BUT EMPTY, JUST THE WAY VI LIKED IT. This was her time to be away from the chaos of her life and take an inventory of the week's events. She called it Grocery Therapy. The canned vegetable aisle was for problem solving. The baking aisle was where she found inspiration. And the adult beverage aisle was where she made promises to herself and cemented future plans. On this night, Vi went home to celebrate.

ARRANGE AN OVEN RACK in the lowest position and place a baking sheet on it to catch drips. Heat your oven to 450°F.

TO MAKE THE FILLING: In a medium saucepan, combine all of the ingredients. Heat your filling over medium heat until bubbly, stirring occasionally.

TO MAKE THE CRUSTS: Butter three 5-by-$1\frac{1}{2}$-inch individual pot pie pans.

IN A SMALL BOWL, stir together the biscuit mix and water. On a lightly floured surface, knead your dough several times. Pat the dough flat and roll very thin, as you would for a pie crust. Cut out six $4\frac{1}{2}$-inch rounds. Place one round of dough in each pan. Press the dough into the bottom and about two-thirds up the sides of each pan. Scoop about 1 cup of the hot filling over each bottom crust. Top each with a round of dough. Cut a little X in the center of each top crust. Brush the top crusts with a little of your beaten egg mixture. Bake the pies on the baking sheet at 450°F for 20 minutes, or until the pies are shiny-topped and bubbly. Serve right in the pans or invert onto serving plates.

St. Anthony's

ROSEMARY BRAISED RABBIT

—⟫⟫⟫ ❈ ⟪⟪⟪—

MAKES DINNER FOR TWO

One (approx. 3 lb) dressed rabbit, cut into six pieces (see Note)

1/2 cup whole-grain Creole mustard

2 Tbsp chopped fresh rosemary, divided, plus some sprigs for garnish

1/4 cup olive oil

1/2 medium red onion, roughly chopped

2 stalks celery, roughly chopped (about 3/4 cup)

2 parsnips, peeled and cut into 1 in chunks (about 1 1/2 cups)

4 colorful carrots, peeled and cut into 1 in chunks (about 1 1/2 cups)

1/4 cup Sauternes

2 cups vegetable broth or rabbit broth

4 cups cooked rice grits (see page 34) or slightly overcooked short-grain white rice

1/4 tsp toasted caraway seeds

MILDRED WAS PLUM TORE UP ABOUT LOSING HER CAMEO PIN. It was a family heirloom, and she couldn't bear the thought of having to tell her sister that it had gone missing. Every morning for the last week and a half, Mildred prayed to St. Anthony, hoping it would turn up. But in her dreams, the patron saint of lost things started losing things of his own. Why just last night, St. Anthony lost his lucky rabbit's foot while trimming the rosemary hedge. This had her worried.

〰〰〰〰〰〰〰〰〰〰〰〰〰〰〰〰〰〰〰〰〰

RUB YOUR RABBIT PIECES all over with the mustard and sprinkle with 1 Tbsp of the rosemary. Refrigerate, uncovered, for about 2 hours or up to 8.

WHEN READY TO BRAISE YOUR RABBIT, heat your oven to 325°F.

HEAT A LARGE PAELLA PAN OR DUTCH OVEN OVER MEDIUM HEAT, then add the oil. When the oil is pretty hot, place the rabbit pieces a few at a time in the oil and cook for 2 to 3 minutes undisturbed, or until browned and the meat releases easily from the pan. Gently turn the pieces and cook for 2 minutes more. Take the rabbit from the pot and set it aside. Add your onion, celery, parsnips, carrots, remaining 1 Tbsp rosemary, and Sauternes to the pot and scrape up any brown bits. Add the broth and return the rabbit to the pot. Raise the heat to medium-high and bring to a boil. Cover the pot and put it in the oven. Cook the rabbit in the oven at 325°F for 50 minutes. Remove the lid and cook for about 10 minutes more. Garnish with rosemary sprigs and serve with rice grits strewn with caraway seeds.

NOTIONS & NOTES
—◆◆◆—

TO BUTCHER A RABBIT

Basically what you are going to do is remove the hind legs by cutting through the spot where the legs join the spine. Then turn and yank the legs off. They will be in the shape of a pair of pants. Separate the legs. Then cut under and around the front legs as you would chicken wings, removing them from the rib cage. Next, right below the rib cage you are going to separate the "saddle" (the pair of loins). Do this by cutting right below the ribs and removing the meaty section by cutting through the spine and under the rib cage. (Save the rib section to use for stock in place of the vegetable broth, if you are really committed.) Then cut the saddle into two pieces, crosswise through the backbone. This will yield six pieces of rabbit to be braised and a rib section and scraps to use to make stock. You can also ask your butcher to cut up the rabbit.

Frank's
COLLARD GREEN AND FIELD PEA FRIED RICE

❧ ❈ ❧

MAKES DINNER FOR FOUR

3 Tbsp bacon grease
or peanut oil, divided

2 Tbsp peeled grated
fresh ginger

¼ tsp red pepper flakes,
or more to taste

1 Tbsp chopped garlic

½ cup chopped white onion

½ cup chopped celery

One 15 oz can field peas
with snaps, drained and rinsed

6 cups (about 1 bunch) stemmed
collard greens cut into ribbons

2 cups cooked and cooled
long-grain white rice

1 Tbsp rice vinegar

1 Tbsp soy sauce,
or more to taste

1 tsp sesame oil,
or more to taste

2 large eggs, beaten with
a pinch of kosher salt and
finely ground black pepper

Toasted sesame seeds for garnish

FRANK HAD BEEN A REGULAR AT THE CARNIVAL FOR YEARS, SPENDING HIS MONEY WITH THE SAME CROOKED-EYED CARNY, BOUND AND DETERMINED TO WIN. But, after so many failed attempts, playing against chance had become more of a habit than anything else. This time, though, he had a secret weapon: Lottie. They'd only been dating for a month, but he knew she was his good luck charm. He was right. Finally, Frank won a lion at the ring toss.

〜〜〜〜〜〜

HEAT A WOK OR A VERY LARGE SKILLET over the hottest burner on the stove for several minutes, until it is really hot. Add 2 Tbsp of your bacon grease and heat it for a few seconds. Swirl the grease around the wok, then add your ginger and red pepper flakes and cook for 30 seconds. Add your garlic, onion, celery, and field peas with snaps. Cook for 1 minute, then stir. Toss in your greens and cook for 1 minute. Push everything over to one side. Add the remaining 1 Tbsp bacon grease to the bare part of the skillet. Add your rice to the blank spot and let it cook undisturbed for 1 minute. Add the vinegar and soy sauce. Toss everything together. Push everything to one side of the wok and pour your sesame oil in the blank spot. Pour your eggs onto the sesame oil. When the eggs begin to set, chop them up and toss with everything else in the pan. Sprinkle sesame seeds over the fried rice. Season with additional soy sauce, sesame oil, and red pepper flakes, if desired.

WE LIKE TO USE

Missimati Bayou Bouquet
rice from Two Brooks Farm in
Sumner, Mississippi.

Agnes's
SQUASH
BLOSSOMS

>>> ❄ <<<

MAKES BLOSSOMS FOR FOUR

1 cup crumbled queso blanco

2 Tbsp Duchess's Mayonnaise
(see page 13) or store-bought
mayonnaise

1 tsp freshly squeezed
lime juice

$\frac{1}{2}$ tsp grated lime zest

2 Tbsp chopped fresh basil

1 Tbsp chopped
fresh flat-leaf parsley

$\frac{1}{4}$ tsp fine sea salt

$\frac{1}{4}$ tsp finely ground
black pepper

12 squash blossoms

2 large eggs

1 cup panko or regular
bread crumbs

AGNES LOVED COMBING MAYONNAISE THROUGH HER CURLS. It reminded her of the summers she spent with her grandmother Doreen in Texas. At night, they'd sit in front of the console television, watching old movies and doing each other's hair. Grandmother Doreen swore by mayo for her curls and Crisco for her feet.

LINE A BAKING SHEET with aluminum foil or parchment paper. Heat your oven to 400°F. In a small bowl, mix together the cheese, mayonnaise, lime juice, lime zest, basil, and parsley. Season with the salt and pepper.

CAREFULLY SPOON YOUR FILLING into the squash blossoms and loosely twist the ends of the petals to seal. Lightly beat the eggs in a medium bowl and put the bread crumbs in a pie pan. Dip each stuffed squash blossom in egg, then bread crumbs, and place a few inches apart on the baking sheet. Bake at 400°F for 10 minutes, or until lightly browned and crispy. Let the blossoms cool for a couple of minutes before serving.

NOTIONS & NOTES
◆◆◆

QUESO BLANCO
is a fresh cheese simply made with cow's milk and vinegar.

SQUASH ARE SO PROLIFIC
in the summer, there are plenty of blooms for you to pinch.
You will hardly notice a drop in your squash crop.

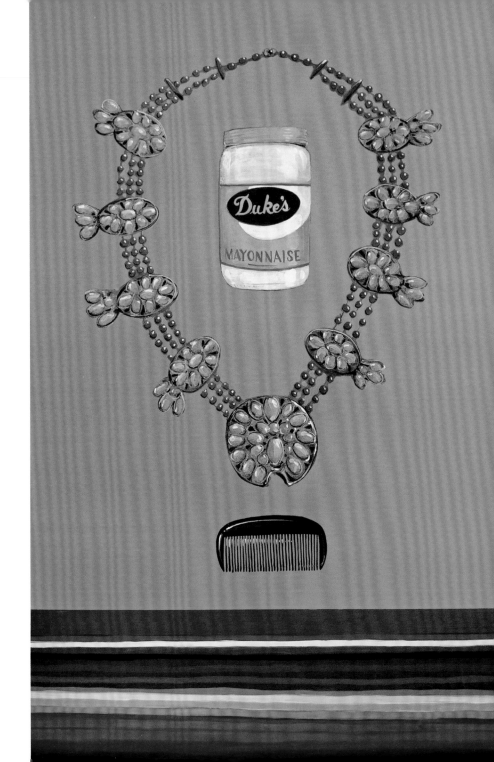

THESE ARE QUITE NICE

served with Lenore Anne's Delta
Hot Tamale Balls (page 82) and
a simple salad for dinner.

Cordelia's
CORNISH HENS

→→→ ❄ ←←←

1 cup pomegranate molasses

¼ cup balsamic vinegar

¼ cup olive oil

4 garlic cloves,
very finely chopped

1 Tbsp chopped fresh rosemary,
plus sprigs for garnish

Pinch of red pepper flakes

Four Cornish game hens
(approx. 1½ lb each)

Kosher salt and coarsely ground
black pepper

2 shallots, peeled and halved

Pomegranate seeds for garnish,
if desired

CORDELIA WANTED FLOWERS ON HER BIRTHDAY CAKE INSTEAD OF CANDLES. She had stopped counting the years anyway. She was throwing her own party for once, so she was more than ready to do it her way. And besides, the last of the zinnias could use some thinning. A shock of color would really make her favorite chocolate cake look like the celebration it's meant to inspire. Her guests were on their way, so Cordelia took supper out of the oven and set out through the screen door with her pruning shears.

〜〜〜〜〜〜〜〜〜〜〜〜〜〜〜〜〜

IN A SMALL BOWL, make a simple marinade with your pomegranate molasses, vinegar, oil, garlic, chopped rosemary, and red pepper flakes. Set aside one-quarter of your marinade for basting. Place the rest of the marinade in a large container with your hens. Marinate the birds for at least 30 minutes or up to 2 hours in the refrigerator, flipping them over a couple of times to coat the birds.

HEAT YOUR OVEN TO 400°F.

REMOVE THE HENS FROM THE MARINADE and discard the marinade. Season the birds with salt and pepper. Tuck a shallot half into each hen. Tie up the legs with twine. Set your hens breast-side up in a low-sided roasting pan or rimmed baking sheet with the legs facing the corners. Tuck the wing tips under the backs of the birds. Leave as much space as possible between the birds so they brown evenly. Roast at 400°F, basting with your reserved marinade, for 50 minutes to 1 hour, until they are a deep golden brown and a thermometer registers 165°F when stuck into the thickest part and not touching the bone. You may want to rotate the pan halfway through cooking, to ensure that the hens cook evenly.

LET THE HENS REST FOR 15 MINUTES BEFORE SERVING, drizzled with pan juices. Garnish with rosemary sprigs and pomegranate seeds, if desired.

IF YOU REALLY WANT TO
show out for a dinner party,
serve these hens as an entrée
with spoonbread (page 102),
steamed asparagus, and
Flannery's Gracious Coffee
Fudge Cake (page 147)
for dessert.

5

Sam's
SMOKED PORK CHOP AND APPLE PIE

❦

**MAKES ONE 9 IN
SAVORY PIE**

4 tart apples (about 2 lb), such as Braeburn or Winesap, cored and cut into 1/2 in pieces

2 Tbsp finely chopped Vidalia or other sweet onion

1 lb boneless smoked pork chops, trimmed of fat and cut into 1 in pieces

2 Tbsp cornstarch

1 Tbsp apple brandy, if desired

1 tsp poultry seasoning (see Note)

1/4 tsp coarsely ground black pepper, plus a little to sprinkle on top

One 17.3 oz package frozen puff pastry, thawed

1 egg white, beaten with 1 Tbsp water

Sharp Cheddar cheese for serving (if desired, see Note)

SAM KNEW THAT WATERING PLANTS MADE THEM GROW, SO HE THOUGHT HE MIGHT BE ABLE TO GROW MORE PIE. But, of course, Sissy ran outside to tell him otherwise. Sam was so tired of her ruining his fun. He let Sissy have her say, and then he walked over to the garden hose to fill up the watering can.

GET A LARGE BOWL AND TOSS TOGETHER YOUR APPLES, onion, pork, cornstarch, brandy (if desired), poultry seasoning, and pepper.

ON A LIGHTLY FLOURED COUNTERTOP, roll out each piece of dough to a 14-inch square. Ease one pastry square into a 9½-inch deep-dish pie pan. Pour all of the filling over this bottom crust. Lay the other piece of dough on top. Press the edges together to seal and trim the overhang to 1 inch. Save the scraps of dough. Crimp the edge decoratively and cut a few slits on top for venting steam. Brush the top crust of your pie with the beaten egg white and sprinkle with a bit of black pepper. Make decorations with dough scraps on the top of your pie, and brush them with the egg white. Put your pie in the freezer while heating the oven.

HEAT YOUR OVEN TO 400°F. Place a rimmed baking sheet on the middle rack to heat as the oven comes to temperature. When the oven is ready, place the pie on the baking sheet in the oven. Bake for 30 minutes, or until the crust is just turning golden. Lower the oven temperature to 375°F and bakefor 40 minutes more, or until the top is deeply browned and your filling is really bubbling. Transfer the pie to a wire rack to cool slightly before serving.

TO MAKE YOUR OWN POULTRY SEASONG:

Combine equal amounts dried thyme, sage, marjoram, and rosemary.

Add a little grated nutmeg.

Anytime SWEETS

Lucille's
LEMON LAVENDER FLOAT

➤➤➤ ❉ ◄◄◄

MAKES FLOATS FOR FOUR

1 cup heavy cream

1½ tsp dried lavender flowers, plus extra for garnish

2 Tbsp powdered sugar

⅛ tsp vanilla extract

1 pt lemon sorbet

2 cups lavender lemonade sparkling soda

Golden rum, if desired

CHICAGO, 1932. It was snowing outside, so Lucille drew herself a bath. It was late in the year for this kind of weather, and the moon was full. Certainly, she figured, this coincidence might portend calamitous events to come. So Lucille lit a candle, poured a nip of rum, placed three drops of lavender in the bath, and called on the spirits to guide her.

~~~~~~~~~~~~~~

CHILL FOUR TALL SERVING GLASSES. In a small saucepan, bring your cream and lavender to a simmer. Remove from the heat and let steep for 15 minutes. Strain your cream into a medium bowl and discard the flowers. Chill the cream until very cold. Add the powdered sugar and vanilla. In a large bowl with an electric mixer or a whisk, whip the cream until it forms soft peaks.

SCOOP ½ CUP SORBET INTO EACH GLASS and pour about ½ cup lemonade over the sorbet. Add a splash of rum, if desired. Top with a dollop of your whipped lavender cream and a tiny sprinkle of dried flowers. Serve with iced tea spoons and fat paper straws.

LOOK FOR

French-style sparkling lemonade in stopper-topped glass bottles.

BE SURE

your lavender is for culinary use.

Ruth's
KEY LIME FRAPPÉ

**MAKES MILK SHAKES
FOR FOUR**

¹/₄ cup sweetened condensed milk

¹/₄ cup Marshmallow Fluff

¹/₂ cup whole milk

2 cups vanilla ice cream

2 cups lime sherbet

1 Tbsp graham cracker crumbs,
plus additional
for garnish

3 Tbsp Key lime juice, fresh or
bottled

1 tsp grated Key lime
or regular lime zest,
plus additional for garnish

Sweetened whipped cream
for garnish, if desired

RUTH LOVED THE BEACH AND KEY LIME PIE. It had been ages since she experienced either, but every time she stood at the sink, she took a moment to glance over at the postcard she kept from her days in Florida. It sat right next to the sand painting she brought back from Arizona. It was a dream come true when her local grocery started selling Key lime juice by the bottle back in '68. Ruth always kept at least two bottles at the ready.

PUT YOUR SWEETENED CONDENSED MILK, Fluff, milk, ice cream, sherbet, graham cracker crumbs, lime juice, and lime zest in your blender and blend until thick and bubbly. Pour into four tall glasses. Top with whipped cream, if desired, and a sprinkling of lime zest and crumbs.

NOTIONS & NOTES

**FOR A NICELY FESTIVE
TROPICAL GARNISH,**
poke two of Lessie's
Forgotten Coconut
Meringues (page 133)
down into your frappé.

Elise's
ANGEL FOOD CAKE WITH RASPBERRY CURD

⟩⟩⟩ ❄ ⟨⟨⟨

**MAKES ONE 10 IN
CAKE RING**

CAKE

12 large egg whites, at room
temperature (reserve 8 yolks for
the raspberry curd)

1 tsp cream of tartar

1 tsp vanilla extract

$^1/_4$ tsp fine sea salt

$1^1/_3$ cups granulated unrefined
cane sugar

1 cup cake flour

ELISE DID WANT SOMETHING DIFFERENT; SHE WANTED A PIECE OF CAKE. But her grandmother insisted on making her signature birthday Jell-O mold. Again. It was pretty, she had to admit, but she simply couldn't abide the texture. Elise longed for a beautiful cake—any kind of cake would do—with dainty florets covering the top and a thick layer of raspberry hidden inside. But she didn't dare hurt her grandmother's feelings. So Elise enjoyed the party, as well as the birthday Jell-O mold, biding her time before she could enjoy the contraband cake hidden in the hatbox at the top of her bedroom closet.

〰〰〰〰〰〰〰〰〰〰〰

TO MAKE THE CAKE: Heat your oven to 350°F. In a large bowl with an electric mixer, whip your egg whites, cream of tartar, vanilla, and salt at medium-low speed until they begin to change from clear to opaque. Increase the speed to medium. When you see the beaters leave distinct trails through the whites, it is time to increase the speed to high. With the mixer running, slowly pour in the sugar. Continue to whip until medium-stiff peaks form. Be careful not to overwhip your whites. You don't want them to be broken or too stiff. When the peaks are perky and just slightly limp over at the top when you lift the beaters, you are there. This allows the whites to swell nicely when baked and give the cake a lovely crumb.

SIFT $^1/_3$ CUP OF THE FLOUR OVER YOUR WHIPPED EGG WHITES. Gently fold in the flour with a large flexible spatula until just incorporated. Repeat twice with the remaining flour, $^1/_3$ cup at a time, making sure to get the spatula down to the very bottom of the bowl. Fold the batter until you don't see any pockets of flour.

SPOON YOUR BATTER into an ungreased large angel food cake pan or 10-inch tube pan. Bake at 350°F for 40 to 45 minutes, until the cake is golden and well risen and springs back when touched lightly. Immediately invert your cake but leave it in the pan. Let it cool completely.

Continued

RASPBERRY CURD

One 12 oz package frozen raspberries, thawed and mashed

1 cup granulated unrefined cane sugar

8 large egg yolks

¼ cup freshly squeezed lemon juice

Pinch of fine sea salt

10 Tbsp (1¼ sticks) cold unsalted butter, cut into tablespoon-size pieces

FOR SERVING

Fresh raspberries

Sweetened whipped cream, if desired

TO MAKE THE RASPBERRY CURD: Press the berries through a mesh strainer and into a small heavy-bottomed saucepan, reserving the juice and discarding the seeds and pulp. Whisk your sugar, egg yolks, lemon juice, and salt into the raspberry juice. Add the butter. Cook over medium heat while continuously whisking. Heat for 5 minutes, or until the curd just begins to bubble. It will thicken as it cools. Pour the curd into a container and press food wrap against the surface to prevent a skin from forming or rub a little cold butter over the surface to make a film.

LOOSEN THE CAKE FROM THE EDGES and center of the pan with a long, sharp, thin knife. Be sure to use a serrated or angel food cake knife with a sawing motion to cut the cake. Serve with raspberry curd, fresh raspberries, and, if using, whipped cream.

NOTIONS & NOTES

◆◆◆

USE YOUR REMAINING
4 egg yolks to make Etta's Third-Date
Chocolate Brandy Pudding (page 141).

WHEN FOLDING YOUR FLOUR
into your egg whites, use the widest flexible
spatula you have. Be sure to turn the bowl
as you run the spatula around the edges,
dipping down to the bottom of your bowl
and folding the whites over the flour.

IF YOUR CAKE PAN RESTS FLAT
on the counter when inverted, set it
with the center of the pan on a can to let
air circulate and keep your cake
from sweating and weeping.

AN ANTIQUE STERLING SILVER
angel food cake knife, along with a copy
of this recipe and a baked angel food
cake, makes for a lovely hostess gift.

Velma's
SECRET ICE CREAM SUNDAE

>>> ❊ <<<

**MAKES ABOUT 1 QT
ICE CREAM**

ICE CREAM

6 large egg yolks

³/₄ cup maple syrup

1 cup heavy cream

1¹/₂ cups half-and-half

1 tsp kosher salt

SUNDAES

Maple syrup

Crushed dill pickle–flavored
potato chips

Crisp bacon bits

NOTIONS & NOTES

◆ ━ ◆ ◆ ◆ ━ ◆

USE AMBER RICH
or darker grade maple syrup,
sometimes labeled Grade B,
for this ice cream, if you
can get ahold of some. It
will give your ice cream the
strongest maple flavor.

**VELMA'S MOTHER-IN-LAW HAD BEEN
PRESSING HER FOR GRANDCHILDREN.**
When she walked into the kitchen
at midnight and found Velma eating
pickles and ice cream, she knew
her mother-in-law couldn't help
but put two and two together. Yes,
Velma had a secret: she was having
twins. But she'd wait two more
months before letting the cat out
of the bag.

〰〰〰〰〰

TO MAKE THE ICE CREAM: In a medium
heavy-bottomed saucepan, whisk together
your egg yolks, maple syrup, cream, and
half-and-half, then set over medium-low
heat. Stirring frequently, cook until a thin
custard coats the back of a spoon and a
finger swiped through leaves a clean line,
10 to 15 minutes. Stir in the salt. Pour into
a storage container with a lid. Refrigerate,
covered, for at least 6 hours.

CHURN THE CUSTARD in an ice cream maker
according to the manufacturer's instructions. Place the ice cream in an airtight
container and, on a good day, freeze for at
least 3 hours before serving. On the rest of
the days, just start scooping sundaes out.

TO MAKE A SUNDAE, scoop some ice cream
into a bowl, drizzle it with a little maple
syrup, and sprinkle with a tiny bit of chips
and bacon.

Francesca's
MILK AND HONEY CAKE

➤➤➤ ❋ ⤙⤙⤙

**MAKES ONE 8 IN
SQUARE CAKE**

½ cup whole milk

½ cup honey

½ tsp almond extract

2 cups unbleached
all-purpose flour

2½ tsp baking powder

½ tsp fine sea salt

½ cup (1 stick) unsalted butter,
at room temperature

½ cup granulated unrefined
cane sugar

2 large eggs

Powdered sugar for dusting,
if desired

FRANCESCA'S MOTHER ALWAYS SAID THAT HONEY WAS NATURE'S MIRACLE, SO SHE THOUGHT IT MIGHT BE JUST THE THING TO FIX HER BROKEN DOLL. She also believed that pillowcase openings facing the center of the bed would bring the house down.

HEAT YOUR OVEN TO 350°F. Butter an 8-inch square baking dish and set it aside.

IN A BOWL, COMBINE YOUR MILK, HONEY, AND ALMOND EXTRACT. In a separate bowl, whisk together your flour, baking powder, and salt.

IN A LARGE BOWL WITH AN ELECTRIC MIXER, beat the butter at medium speed for 2 minutes, or until creamy. Gradually add the granulated sugar and beat for 4 minutes more, or until light and fluffy. Add the eggs one at a time, letting the first fully incorporate before adding the next. Turn the speed to low and alternately add the milk mixture and the flour mixture. Beat just until your batter is smooth. Scrape your batter into the prepared dish and bake at 350°F for 50 minutes, or until the cake springs back when touched lightly and a toothpick inserted into the center comes out clean. Let cool, then slice and serve with a dusting of powdered sugar, if desired.

NOTIONS & NOTES

◆◆◆

SLICES OF THIS CAKE
are quite wonderful for
breakfast, toasted and served
with raspberry curd (page 126).

THIS CAKE TAKES WELL
to all sorts of additions of fruits
and nuts and makes a
lovely foundation for trifles
or petit fours.

francesca

5.

Lessie's
FORGOTTEN COCONUT MERINGUES

⟶⟫⟫ ❄ ⟪⟪⟵

MAKES TWENTY-FOUR CRISP MERINGUES

3 large egg whites

6 Tbsp granulated unrefined cane sugar

¼ tsp fine sea salt

1 tsp vanilla extract

½ cup sweetened coconut flakes, divided

LESSIE TWIST-TIED HER WEDDING RINGS TO HER BRA STRAP. She learned her lesson the last time she made meringue. Lessie separated the eggs over the sink and, while cradling a yolk in her hand, both rings just slipped right off. She ended up wasting half a day with her head up under her least favorite cabinet, working to fish them out of the drain trap. She couldn't let that happen again.

〰〰〰〰〰

HEAT YOUR OVEN TO 200°F. In a large bowl with an electric mixer, whip your egg whites on low speed until they are frothy. When the whites start to turn opaque, gradually increase the speed to high. Slowly and steadily add the sugar and salt with your mixer running. Continue to whip until the whites are stiff and glossy. The beaters will leave a very distinct trail through the egg whites and the peak will stand tall and erect when the beaters are lifted. Fold in your vanilla and ¼ cup of your coconut.

TAKE A BAKING SHEET and put small dots of meringue in the corners and a couple in the center. These dots will anchor your parchment paper and keep it from lifting up while you pipe the meringues. Line the baking sheet with parchment.

WITH A LARGE PASTRY BAG fitted with a large open star or round tip, pipe your meringue into 3-inch-long bars about 2 inches apart on the parchment. (You can also use a piping bag with a ½-inch opening and no tip.) Sprinkle with the remaining ¼ cup coconut and bake at 200°F for 1 hour, or until the meringues are crisp on the outside. Turn off the oven and let the meringues dry completely in the oven until crisp through and through, about 3 hours or overnight, if need be (as long as it is not raining or too humid). Store the cooled meringues in an airtight container.

NOTIONS & NOTES

◆◆◆

IF YOUR MERINGUES seem to not want to let go of the parchment, lightly wipe your counter with a damp rag. Place the paper on the damp surface and let it sit for 2 minutes. The meringues should then lift right off.

THESE CRISP COCONUT MERINGUES are nice plunged into Etta's Third-Date Chocolate Brandy Pudding (page 141), which uses up the egg yolks left from separating your whites.

Johnny's
SKATING RINK
MINTS

MAKES ABOUT TEN
DOZEN CANDIES

½ cup (1 stick) top-quality salted butter, at room temperature

One 3 oz package cream cheese, at room temperature

5½ cups powdered sugar, sifted, divided, plus a tiny bit extra for dusting

1 Tbsp heavy cream

1 tsp pure spearmint extract, or 2 drops peppermint oil

Pale green paste food coloring, if desired

JOHNNY COMBED HIS HAIR, THEN DABBED SOME MINT EXTRACT ON HIS NECK. He loved smelling like candy. His Tee-Momma was making mints for the Missionary Society's Sunday Luncheon. But it was Friday, and Johnny was going to the skating rink.

LINE SEVERAL BAKING SHEETS OR TRAYS with waxed paper, parchment paper, or aluminum foil. In a large bowl with an electric mixer, beat your butter and cream cheese together on low speed, scraping the sides and beaters often, until the mixture is smooth and creamy. With the mixer running, gradually add 5 cups of the powdered sugar. Beat in the cream and spearmint extract. Continue beating on low speed for 3 minutes, or until a soft dough is formed. Beat in the food coloring, if using. Add the remaining ½ cup sugar, 2 Tbsp at a time, if the dough seems unmanageable.

ON A WORK SURFACE DUSTED WITH A BIT OF POWDERED SUGAR, knead your dough until smooth. Divide the dough into fourths and roll each section into a 1½-inch-diameter rope. Cut small ½-inch pillows from the rope and place the pillows on the baking sheets. Repeat with the remaining dough. Allow the mint pillows to sit uncovered and undisturbed to air-dry for 2 days, or until the surface is dry. Store the dried mints between layers of waxed paper in an airtight container.

NOTIONS & NOTES

PLAN AHEAD
and package these up in pretty little bags by the handful and send them home with guests of any sort: dinner, shower, birthday, or drop-in.

Matilda's
LONG-LASTING GRANDE FOURS

————»»» ❄ «««————

MAKES TWO ICED LOAF CAKES

CAKES

Two 1 lb store-bought
pound cakes, or a double batch of
Francesca's Milk and Honey Cake
(page 130) baked in two 8 by 4 by
2$\frac{1}{2}$ in loaf pans, cooled

$\frac{1}{2}$ cup pineapple preserves

ICING

3 cups powdered sugar

1 Tbsp light corn syrup

$\frac{1}{4}$ tsp almond extract

$\frac{1}{4}$ tsp vanilla extract

$\frac{1}{4}$ cup white chocolate chips

MATILDA WANTED TO REMEMBER THIS NIGHT FOREVER, SO SHE COVERED THE PETIT FOURS WITH HAIRSPRAY WHEN SHE GOT HOME. As soon as they were dry, she put them in the medicine cabinet and then took a long look in the mirror. Matilda shook and shook that hairspray can like she was mad at it. She needed to get the last spritz for herself before leaving for her next engagement. Matilda's dance card was always full.

TO ASSEMBLE THE CAKES: With a serrated knife, cut away the crust of your cakes, removing as little of the cake as possible. Trim the sides to make naked, straight-sided rectangular cakes. To ease cutting the cake into layers, turn your cake so the longest side is against your cutting board. Slice vertically through the cake, making three long lengthwise pieces. These will form your cake layers when stacked. Place your cake pieces flat on your work surface, making sure to keep them in order and right-side up. Spread the bottom layer of each cake with a very thin coating of pineapple preserves and carefully place the center cake layer over the preserves, making sure to even up the sides. Spread this layer with a very thin coating of preserves and top with the last layer of cake. Tidy up the sides. Wrap the cakes and place in the freezer while you make your icing. (Save the cake scraps to toast and crumble over ice cream another day.)

PLACE A WIRE RACK OVER A RIMMED BAKING SHEET to catch drips and collect the icing for the second round of glazing your cakes. Set your cakes on top.

TO MAKE THE ICING: In a medium heat-proof bowl set over (but not touching) simmering water or a double boiler, whisk together the powdered sugar, $\frac{1}{4}$ cup water, the corn syrup, and extracts. Cook over simmering water until your glaze is smooth and slowly drizzles off your whisk. Stir in the white chocolate chips until they are completely melted into the icing. A good temperature for working with your icing will be between 90°F and 100°F, or about as warm as a baby's bottle. Working while your icing is warm, spoon the icing over the top and sides of one cake. Gather the icing that accumulated on the sheet pan and warm it again. Repeat with your second cake. Once the icing is no longer dripping, transfer the cakes to serving platters. You may need to use a sharp knife to loosen the hardened glaze from the rack.

NOTIONS & NOTES

IT IS IMPORTANT
that the jam layer is very thin so it does not ooze or seep out from between the cake layers when iced. If the jam seems to be dragging or tearing the cake, warm the jam with a little bit of water to ease spreading.

WE HAVE FOUND
that generic, or store-brand, powdered sugar can have an overtly cornstarchy taste. Use a quality brand you trust.

DECORATE
these oversized petit fours with edible flowers, nonpareils, or royal icing decors.

IF YOU EVER FIND YOURSELF

in Houston, Texas, we recommend making a special trip to Moeller's Bakery, a family operation that has been supplying the city with delicious cakes, pies, cheese straws, orange rolls, and more since 1930. Their perfect petit fours are the stuff of legend. When in Mississippi, stop in at Campbell's Bakery, located in the happening Fondren neighborhood of Jackson. Since 1962, they've been piping rosettes of any color requested on top of their dainty cakes.

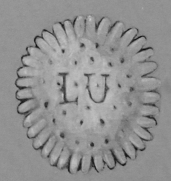

Lena's COFFEE SHORTBREAD

MAKES EIGHTEEN COOKIES

1 cup (2 sticks) unsalted butter, at room temperatuer

½ cup granulated unrefined cane sugar

½ tsp very finely ground coffee or espresso beans

⅛ tsp fine sea salt

1¾ cups unbleached all-purpose flour

¼ cup white or brown rice flour

NOTIONS & NOTES

THESE SANDY SHORTBREAD cookies pair wonderfully with Loretta's Café con Mitad y Mitad (page 21).

LENA WAS HAVING ONE OF HER SPELLS. She knew the only way out of it was to press her best linens and call the girls. So Lena put on some coffee and set the table for guests. She was going to have to ask Loretta to pick up the half-and-half because she was plum out. She might have to ask her to spring for two pints so that they could take their time sorting through it all.

HEAT YOUR OVEN TO 325°F. In a large bowl with an electric mixer, cream your butter, sugar, coffee, and salt for several minutes, until light and fluffy. Gradually beat in the flours. Beat for a minute or two, until you have a smooth dough. Press your dough into an ungreased 9-inch square baking pan. Prick with a fork about every inch or so.

BAKE AT 325°F FOR 40 TO 45 MINUTES, until light brown with a dry look to the top. Cut into eighteen rectangles while warm (three rows by six columns). Cool completely in the pan on a wire rack. Store your shortbread in a vintage tin.

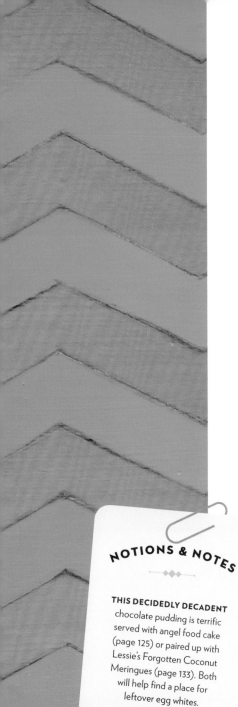

Etta's
THIRD-DATE CHOCOLATE BRANDY PUDDING

→⟩⟩ ❄ ⟨⟨←

MAKES DESSERT FOR FOUR

¹/₄ cup granulated unrefined cane sugar

¹/₄ cup cornstarch

2 Tbsp unsweetened dark cocoa powder

¹/₈ tsp fine sea salt

2 cups whole milk

4 large egg yolks

One 1 in cinnamon stick

2 Tbsp brandy or cognac

2 Tbsp unsalted butter, cut into small pieces

3 oz semisweet chocolate, finely chopped, or ¹/₄ cup chocolate chips

Top-quality maraschino cherries for garnish, if desired

NOTIONS & NOTES

◆◆◆

THIS DECIDEDLY DECADENT chocolate pudding is terrific served with angel food cake (page 125) or paired up with Lessie's Forgotten Coconut Meringues (page 133). Both will help find a place for leftover egg whites.

ETTA DIDN'T WANT TO SEEM PRESUMPTUOUS, BUT SHE WENT AHEAD AND PREPARED HER SPECIAL DARK CHOCOLATE PUDDING THAT MORNING. While it was setting, she changed the sheets, and then went out to do her afternoon errands. She didn't know how the date was going to go but, in the end, Etta invited him up for dessert.

〜〜〜〜

IN A MEDIUM HEAVY-BOTTOMED POT, whisk together your sugar, cornstarch, cocoa powder, and salt. Slowly whisk in the milk, then the egg yolks. Add the cinnamon stick and place the pot over medium heat.

COOK WHILE STIRRING UNCEASINGLY with a flexible heat-proof spatula, being sure to get the sides and bottom of the pot, until your pudding is very thick, 6 to 7 long minutes. Add your brandy. Continue to cook for 1 minute at a low, slow, lava-like boil to cook out any remaining starchy flavor and mellow the brandy. Discard the cinnamon stick. Add your butter and chocolate and stir until melted. Spoon the pudding into a bowl. Press a piece of food wrap directly on the surface of the pudding and refrigerate it for at least 2 hours. Serve the pudding in coupes garnished with cherries, if desired.

2 oz

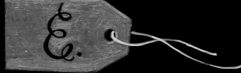

AMERICAN
BEAUTY

USDA

8 oz   BUTTER

NOTIONS & NOTES

◆◆◆

WE LIKE TO USE A BAKING SPRAY
like Baker's Joy that has both oil and
flour in it. It gets into nooks and
crannies and helps seal in crumbs.

IF SO INCLINED, WHEN YOUR CAKE
comes out of the oven and while it is still in
the pan, poke holes down into the cake with a
skewer. Then slowly pour some of the warm
glaze over the cake, letting it sink into the cake.

WE LIKE TO SAVE SOME OF THIS GLAZE TO POUR OVER ICE CREAM AND FRESH FRUIT.

Estelle's
BUTTERSCOTCH POUND CAKE

➤➤➤ ❋ ❰❰❰

**MAKES ONE
VERY LARGE CAKE**

CAKE

$^1/_3$ cup Scotch whisky

$1^1/_4$ cups heavy cream,
at room temperature

1 tsp vanilla extract

$3^1/_2$ cups cake flour

$1^1/_4$ tsp baking powder

$^3/_4$ tsp baking soda

1 tsp fine sea salt

$1^1/_4$ cups ($2^1/_2$ sticks) unsalted
butter, at room temperature

$1^3/_4$ cups granulated unrefined
cane sugar

$^2/_3$ cup packed light brown sugar

5 large eggs, at room temperature

BUTTERSCOTCH GLAZE

6 Tbsp unsalted butter

$^3/_4$ cup packed light brown sugar

$^1/_2$ tsp fine sea salt

2 Tbsp Scotch whisky

1 tsp vanilla extract

1 cup heavy (whipping) cream

Crushed butterscotch candy disks
for garnish, if desired

ESTELLE WAS GOING TO BAKE A POUND CAKE, BUT SHE DECIDED TO POUR HERSELF A GLASS OF SCOTCH INSTEAD. It had been a long day. But then she thought better of ditching her cake-baking plan. After all, she could let the butter soften while she sat at the kitchen table to check her lottery numbers. She took the butter out of the fridge and then went ahead and poured another glass of Scotch to set on the windowsill for later. Estelle knew well enough to save her second drink until she got the cake in the oven.

〰〰〰〰〰〰〰

TO MAKE THE CAKE: Heat your oven to 350°F. Thoroughly spray a large (12 cup) Bundt or tube cake pan with nonstick baking spray or butter, and lightly flour the pan and knock out any excess flour.

COMBINE YOUR SCOTCH, CREAM, AND VANILLA in a liquid measuring cup with a spout. In a medium bowl, whisk together your flour, baking powder, baking soda, and salt. In a large bowl with an electric mixer, beat your butter on medium speed for 1 minute. Add both sugars and beat at medium-high speed for 5 whole minutes, scraping the bottom and sides of the bowl every so often. Turn the speed to medium-low and add your eggs one at a time, mixing well after each addition. Turn the speed to low and add the flour mixture, alternating with your Scotch mixture, beginning and ending with the flour. Give your bowl one more good scrape around the edges and all the way to the bottom. Mix on low for a few seconds. Scrape your batter into your prepared pan. Drop the pan on the counter two times to keep tunnels from forming in the cake as it bakes. Bake at 350°F for 45 to 50 minutes, until your cake springs back when touched lightly and a wooden skewer inserted into the cake comes out with just a few crumbs attached. Let your cake cool in the pan on a wire rack for 15 minutes. Turn your cake out onto the rack to cool completely. When your cake is cool, put it on a platter.

TO MAKE THE BUTTERSCOTCH GLAZE: This glaze will bubble furiously, so use a large, deep pot. Put your butter, brown sugar, salt, Scotch, vanilla, and cream in the pot and stir over medium heat until the sugar has completely dissolved. Bring to a boil and cook for 5 minutes, or until thick and shiny. Let this glaze cool for 5 minutes off the heat. Pour the glaze over your cake, brushing some all over the sides, too. Sprinkle with crushed butterscotch candies, if desired.

Josephine's
CHOCOLATE OMELET FLAMBÉ

——❀——

**MAKES DESSERT
FOR FOUR TO SIX**

¼ cup heavy cream,
plus 2 Tbsp for serving

2 oz semisweet
chocolate, melted
(about ⅓ cup chocolate chips)

3 Tbsp powdered sugar, plus more
for dusting

Pinch of fine sea salt

6 large eggs, very well beaten

2 Tbsp unsalted butter

½ cup rum

⅓ cup light or dark crème de cacao
or favorite chocolate liqueur

1 oz of courage

EARLIER IN THE DAY, JOSEPHINE CLEANED UP AT THE HALF-OFF HOLIDAY CHOCOLATE SALE AT THE REXALL. Once she had her way with it, it sure wouldn't taste like a bargain. So she decided to cap off the night with a flourish. Josephine threw a little party for herself and served all of her favorite foods.

~~~~~~~~~~~~~~~~~~~~~~~~~

IN A LARGE BOWL WITH AN IMMERSION BLENDER OR WHISK, blend your ¼ cup cream, the melted chocolate, powdered sugar, salt, and eggs. It will look spotty, but will melt together while cooking.

MELT YOUR BUTTER in a large (10 inch) nonstick frying pan over medium heat until the butter starts to get a little foamy. Swirl the pan to coat it with butter. Pour your egg mixture into the pan and swirl it around to even out your eggs. With a flexible spatula, stir until the omelet begins to set. Lift the edges of your omelet, letting the uncooked eggs slip beneath. Turn the heat to medium-low and cook, scooting the pan around to prevent scorching, until the omelet is uniformly set and no longer running, but still soft and wet on top. Starting with the edge in front of the handle, fold the omelet to the center of your pan and repeat with the side furthest from the handle, so the two sides meet in the middle. Tidy it up a bit, if needed. Remove from the heat and let it sit for 30 seconds. Dust with powdered sugar.

NOW, MUSTER YOUR COURAGE. Turn your omelet out by inverting it onto a flameproof glass or stoneware platter. Generously dust the top of your omelet with powdered sugar. Have your rum in one glass and your crème de cacao in a separate glass. Pour the remaining 2 Tbsp cream over the crème de cacao. Take your omelet and your glasses to the table. Pour the rum over the omelet and set it ablaze. As soon as the flames subside, pour the crème de cacao mixture over your omelet and serve your astonished guests.

IF YOU'RE NOT IN THE MOOD
to flambé, serve this sugary
chocolate omelet with raspberry
curd (page 126) or lightly
sweetened whipped cream.

CAMAY

THE SOAP OF BEAUTIFUL WOMEN

Flannery's
GRACIOUS COFFEE FUDGE CAKE

MAKES ONE 8 IN LAYER CAKE

CAKE

2¼ cups unbleached all-purpose flour

2¼ cups unrefined granulated cane sugar

1 cup unsweetened dark cocoa powder

1 Tbsp baking soda

1½ tsp baking powder

1 tsp fine sea salt

1½ cups buttermilk, at room temperature

1 cup strongly brewed coffee, at room temperature

¾ cup canola oil

2 tsp vanilla extract

3 large eggs

DARK COFFEE FUDGE FROSTING

2¼ cups (4½ sticks) unsalted butter, at room temperature

1½ cups powdered sugar

¾ cup unsweetened dark cocoa powder

½ cup strongly brewed coffee, at room temperature

½ cup sour cream

1½ tsp vanilla extract

¼ tsp fine sea salt

10 oz dark chocolate, melted

"I HAVE GIVEN UP TRYING TO BE A GRACIOUS LADY . . . I am going back to raising mandrils." —Flannery O'Connor, in an undated letter to editor Robie Macauley.

TO MAKE THE CAKE: Heat your oven to 350°F. Spray three 8-inch round cake pans with nonstick baking spray or butter them and line the bottoms with parchment paper.

IN A LARGE MIXING BOWL, whisk together your flour, granulated sugar, cocoa powder, baking soda, baking powder, and salt.

IN A MEDIUM BOWL, whisk together your buttermilk, coffee, oil, vanilla, and eggs.

ADD YOUR BUTTERMILK MIXTURE to your flour mixture and whisk until smooth. Divide your batter equally among your cake pans. Bake for 20 to 25 minutes, until a toothpick inserted into the center of a cake comes out clean.

LET YOUR CAKES COOL in the pans on wire racks for 10 minutes, then turn them out onto the racks to cool completely.

TO MAKE THE DARK COFFEE FUDGE FROSTING: In a large bowl with an electric mixer, beat your butter on medium speed until very fluffy, 2 to 3 minutes. Sift your powdered sugar and cocoa powder into a medium bowl.

WHILE MIXING AT VERY LOW SPEED, add the powdered sugar mixture to the butter. Add your coffee, sour cream, vanilla, and salt and mix until well incorporated. Increase the speed to medium and beat for 2 minutes. Add your melted chocolate and beat on medium speed until smooth, about 1 minute.

PUT YOUR FIRST CAKE LAYER ROUNDED-SIDE UP ON A CAKE PLATE. Spread about 1 cup of the frosting evenly over that layer. Put the second cake layer on top and repeat with another layer of frosting. Put the final cake layer on top, rounded-side down.

SPREAD a thin "crumb coat" of frosting all over the cake to seal in any loose crumbs. Refrigerate your cake until the frosting begins to firm up, 15 to 20 minutes. Spread your cake with all of the remaining frosting.

List of Illustrations

COVER

Grace couldn't take any chances. Acrylic on wood panel. 24 by 24 in. 2015.

TITLE PAGE

I have given up trying to be a gracious lady . . . I am going back to raising mandrils. —Flannery O'Connor. Acrylic on wood panel. 24 by 24 in. 2009.

TABLE OF CONTENTS

Tia Esther started the rice. Acrylic on wood panel. 12 by 9 in. 2015.

FOREWORD

Maria's mother taught her how to fry chicken on October 3, 1967. Acrylic on metal. 10 by 12 in. 2015.

CHAPTER ONE: MORNING'S GLORIES

Margie arrived home from the party and decided to fry up some bacon. Acrylic on wood. 10 by 8 in (oval). 2010.

Pearl spiked her drink. Acrylic on wood. 11 by 16 in. 2012.

Marge had her usual breakfast and then she took her usual measurements. Acrylic on wood panel. 24 by 24 in. 2014.

Loretta put the coffee on the stove and then crawled back into bed to find the details of her dreams. Acrylic on wood panel. 13$^1/2$ by 18$^1/4$ in. 2011.

Every morning, Dolores put hot paprika in her water and cucumbers under her eyes. Acrylic on wood panel. 12 by 12 in. 2014.

Good Morning, Sunshine! (Ouida). Acrylic on wood panel. 9 by 6 in. 2010.

Dot was running late, so she threw her breakfast in her purse and headed out the door. Acrylic on wood panel. 12 by 12 in. 2010.

Ethel loved breakfast in bed. Too bad she had to make it for herself. Acrylic on wood panel. 14 by 18 in. 2010.

Francine always ate a doughnut before going to bed. She thought it made her dreams sweet. Acrylic on wood panel. 12 by 8 in. 2010.

Ivy packed her suitcase for the trip. Acrylic on wood panel. 17 by 22 in. 2013.

Ruby read the note again while her country ham was in the skillet. Acrylic on wood panel. 13 by 11$^1/2$ in. 2010.

Things you find at the five and dime: candy necklace and vegetable peeler. (Carrye). Acrylic on wood panel. 12 by 9 in. 2015.

"The meanings of words are serious things, you know," Arturo said . . . after talking all day, he was thirsty for buttermilk. —Eudora Welty, The Shoe Bird, *1964.* Acrylic on wood panel. 12 by 12 in. 2009.

CHAPTER TWO: LINGERING LUNCHES

Thelma loved rhinestones and Cheetos. Acrylic on wood panel. 8$^1/2$ by 6$^1/2$ in (oval). 2010.

Eventually, bottled sunshine just wasn't good enough. (Nora). Acrylic on wood panel. 14$^3/4$ by 9 in. 2007.

Rita's nails were still wet, so she asked Carla to grab the bottle opener. Acrylic on wood panel. 12 by 10 in. 2018.

Nanaline coveted her grandmother's aluminum ware that she kept at the beach house. Acrylic on wood panel. 12 by 12 in. 2018.

Alice thought of Guillermo every time she prayed the rosary or cooked cannellini beans. Acrylic on wood panel. 11 by 9$^1/_2$ in. 2009.

Camille's grandmother loved Duke's mayonnaise and costume jewelry. Acrylic on wood panel. 11$^1/_2$ by 10 in. 2008.

Ida had certain things she took with her when she went fishing. Acrylic on wood panel. 13 by 23 in. 2011.

Gayle finally won the chicken drop contest at Sweet's Lounge. Acrylic on wood panel. 3$^1/_2$ by 3$^3/_4$ in. 2008.

Zelda got home later than she expected. Acrylic on wood panel. 13 by 16 in. 2011.

Eliza had quite a large collection of ceramic birds. Each of them had a favorite food. Polly the Bluebird's was, of course, crackers. Acrylic on wood panel. 7 by 7 in. 2007.

Edna ordered the BBQ special—no pickles, extra pie. Acrylic on wood panel. 16 by 22 in. 2013.

Pauline collected lucky charms. Acrylic on wood panel. 6 by 6 in. 2013.

Because that's what boys are made of. (Ben). Acrylic on wood panel. 6 by 6 in. 2008.

CHAPTER THREE: AFTERNOON PICK-ME-UPS

"My peachicken has one trick: he runs up to anyone holding a cigarette and snatches it away and eats it." —Flannery O'Connor. Acrylic on wood panel. 16$^1/_2$ by 12$^1/_2$ in (oval). 2009.

Maxine stayed in to tend to a few things. Acrylic on wood panel. 24 by 12 in. 2014.

Ferdinand decided to go for a swim. Acrylic with green paper on wood panel. 11 by 11 in. 2007.

Juanita always put fresh peaches in her ginger ale. Acrylic on metal. 10 by 8 in. 2016.

Louise kept her favorite earrings hidden in a sardine can in the cupboard. Acrylic on wood panel. 6 by 8$^3/_4$ in. 2008.

Once Clara and Ben were in New Orleans, they tried everything. Acrylic on wood panel. 6 by 6 in. 2008.

Agnes kept a box of firecrackers under her bed, just in case. Acrylic on wood panel. 6 by 6 in. 2011.

How ya durin'? (Franny). Acrylic on wood panel. 12 by 18 in. 2014.

Lenore Anne never threw a party without Delta tamales on her table. Acrylic on wood panel. 12 by 12 in. 2018.

Grace couldn't take any chances. Acrylic on wood panel. 24 by 24 in. 2015.

A love note for his bay beauty down Apalachicola way. (Joseph). Acrylic on wood panel. 9 by 11$^3/_4$ in. 2007.

Clementine prayed over the queso. Acrylic on metal. 10 by 8 in. 2014.

Georgia Kay always looked forward to snapping beans. Acrylic on wood panel. 12 by 12 in. 2018.

CHAPTER FOUR: DINNER DATES & LATE-NIGHT TAKES

Vera ate her weight in oysters. Acrylic on wood panel. 10 by 8 in (oval). 2011.

Angela ran a bath, lit a cigarette, and read some poetry. Acrylic on wood panel. 24 by 12 in. 2014.

Esther had a midnight snack. Acrylic on wood panel. 6$^1/_2$ by 12 in. 2012.

Fanny kept sunglasses and a handkerchief in her apron pocket. Acrylic on wood panel. 12$^3/_4$ by 11 in. 2007.

Things that go with oysters: cornmeal. (Ula Mae). Acrylic on wood panel. 12 by 12 in. 2016.

Stella had an entire room filled with gold objects that she had collected over the years. One day, she decided to send them all off to friends. Acrylic on wood panel. 6$^1/_4$ by 5$^1/_2$ in. 2009.

Vi went home to celebrate. Acrylic on wood panel. 16 by 24 in. 2012.

St. Anthony lost his lucky rabbit's foot while trimming the rosemary hedge. (Mildred). Acrylic on wood panel. 12 by 11 in. 2007.

Finally, Frank won a lion at the ring toss. Acrylic with gold paper on wood panel. 7$\frac{1}{2}$ by 7 in. 2007.

Agnes loved combing mayonnaise through her curls. Acrylic on wood panel. 24 by 36 in. 2014.

Cordelia wanted flowers on her birthday cake instead of candles. Acrylic on wood panel. 8$\frac{3}{4}$ by 5$\frac{3}{4}$ in. 2009.

Sam knew that watering plants made them grow, so he thought he might be able to grow more pie. Acrylic on wood panel. 9$\frac{1}{4}$ by 11$\frac{1}{2}$ in. 2007.

CHAPTER FIVE: ANYTIME SWEETS

Gladys always put a rabbit's foot in her apron pocket when she made a meringue. Acrylic on wood panel. 9$\frac{1}{2}$ by 12$\frac{1}{2}$ in (oval). 2010.

Chicago, 1932. It was snowing outside, so Lucille drew herself a bath. Acrylic, brown paper, and silver paper on wood panel. 11 by 11 in. 2007.

Ruth loved the beach and Key lime pie. Acrylic on wood panel. 12 by 8 in. 2014.

Elise did want something different; she wanted a piece of cake. Acrylic on wood panel. 9 by 8$\frac{3}{4}$ in. 2009.

Velma had a secret. Acrylic on wood panel. 17 by 26 in. 2011.

Francesca's mother always said that honey was nature's miracle, so she thought it might be just the thing to fix her broken doll. Acrylic and gold paper on wood panel. 14 by 11 in. 2007.

Lessie twist-tied her wedding rings to her bra strap. Acrylic on wood panel. 10 by 12 in. 2018.

Johnny combed his hair, then dabbed some mint extract on his neck. He loved smelling like candy. Acrylic on wood panel. 6 by 5$\frac{3}{4}$ in. 2009.

Matilda wanted to remember this night forever, so she covered the petit fours with hairspray when she got home. Acrylic on wood panel. 12 by 12 in. 2009.

Lena put on some coffee and set the table for guests. Acrylic on wood panel. 16 by 21 in. 2011.

Etta invited him up for dessert. Acrylic on wood panel. 11 by 16 in. 2013.

Estelle was going to bake a pound cake, but she decided to pour herself a glass of Scotch instead. Acrylic on wood panel. 11$\frac{1}{4}$ by 12$\frac{1}{4}$ in. 2007.

Josephine threw a little party for herself and served all of her favorite foods. Acrylic on wood panel. 14 by 21 in. 2011.

I have given up trying to be a gracious lady . . . I am going back to raising mandrils. —Flannery O'Connor. Acrylic on wood panel. 24 by 24 in. 2009.

LIST OF ILLUSTRATIONS

Geraldine spoiled Queenie with sweet pickles. Acrylic on wood panel. 11$\frac{1}{4}$ by 16 in. 2011.

ACKNOWLEDGMENTS

Hazel wore Black Rose perfume because it made her feel mysterious. Acrylic on wood panel. 5 by 6 in. 2010.

INDEX

Ruth dreamt of love and crisp linen. Acrylic on wood panel. 6 by 6 in. 2011.

A HEARTFELT THANKS

Acknowledgments

Bennie Flores Ansell

Lisa Barker

Donald Bender

Joseph Bender

Jane Rule Burdine

Minter Byrd

Karen Carrier

Janis Donnaud

Marshall Lynn Evans

Marcie Cohen Ferris

Jon, Caroline & Daniel Foose

Mike Foose

LeAnne Doss Gault

April Grayson

Cristen Hemmins

Casey Kester Herrin

Mary Hoover

Mary Hartwell Howorth

Holly Lewis Hudley

Mary Beth Lasseter

Ronni Lundy

Katy Vinroot O'Brien

Jill O'Connor

Taylor Bowen Ricketts

Sara Roahen

Elizabeth Schatz

Claire Smith

Molly Fergusson Stuart

Molly Boland Thompson

The Thompson Family

Yolande Van Heerden

Sara Wood

&

Residents of the Mississippi Delta
past, present, and future

Black Rose

2 oz.

AND THANKS TO

Sarah Billingsley   Karen Levy

Mikayla Butchart   Joyce Lin

Kelley Galbreath   Magnolia Molcan

Deanne Katz   Cecilia Santini

Tera Kilip   Cynthia Shannon

Steve Kim   Lizzie Vaughan

Lianna Krisoff

Index

THANK YOU FOR VISITING
WITH ALL OF US.

Please do stay in touch. Drop us a line and some snapshots

of your favorite dishes when you have a minute.

-Amy, Martha, and The Ladies.

P.S. YOU CAN FIND US AT WWW.AGOODMEALISHARDTOFIND.COM.